# ANGLESEY REMEMBERS

## Some of its eminent people

# Anglesey Remembers

## Some of its eminent people

Margaret Hughes

*ISBN: 0-86381-222-2*

*Cover design: Smala, Caernarfon*

*First published in 2000 by*
*Gwasg Carreg Gwalch, 12 Iard yr Orsaf, Llanrwst, Wales LL26 0EH*
℡ *01492 642031* 🖷 *01492 641502*
✆ *books@carreg-gwalch.co.uk Internet: www.carreg-gwalch.co.uk*

*For*
*Geraint, Win, Dylan and Faye*

# Thanks

The author is indebted to many people for the content of this book. To the characters themselves, some of whom have left valuable written evidence counted among the treasures from the past; to those who have already researched and whose findings have been recorded and sometimes published; to Anne Venables and her staff at the Anglesey County Record Office, and Handel Evans and the staff at Llangefni Area Library, whose patience and ever-ready help have been such an encouragement; to the Anglesey Antiquarian Society whose Transactions have provided answers to many queries; and to the generous co-operation of Jan Adams of Anglesey County Council. Photography by J.C. Davies Photography, Llanfawr, Holyhead and Ed. Pari-Jones, Llanfair Pwllgwyngyll.

And, of course, to Myrddin ap Dafydd and his team at Gwasg Carreg Gwalch for their forbearance. Working with them is a pleasure.

*Margaret Hughes*

# Contents

# Introduction

Local government in Anglesey in its several guises over the years, community councils and private bodies have been recognising the achievements of those connected with Anglesey by erecting plaques in their honour.

These are scattered over the island, fixed where possible in places directly associated with the subject – a house, a school or a chapel.

Of necessity, the information carried on the plaques is brief, but behind a terse phrase can lie a story full of incident.

For some, life began very simply but developed into a contribution to humanity world-wide. Others gave their talents to improve the quality of life, in the arts or sciences or place of work, closer to home.

This book sets out to introduce some of the colourful characters so remembered and others to whom, as yet, there is no permanent memorial.

To know Anglesey intimately, one must know its history. To appreciate its history, one must know its people.

# Rhodri Mawr (d.877);
# Owain Gwynedd (1110-1170);
# Llywelyn Fawr (1173-1240)

For over half a millennium, the Welsh court at Aberffraw was the scene of planning of events which moulded the pattern of early Welsh history. Here kings and princes met to confer and to plan strategy; it was a place where successful military action was celebrated and defeat was accepted.

Rhodri Mawr was king of Gwynedd, Powys and Deheubarth. Before he succeeded to the throne he was Prince of Gwynedd, becoming king on the death of his father, Merfyn Frych, in 844. Through the death of his uncle, Cyngen, the lands of Powys were added to Gwynedd in 855, as in 872 were parts of Deheubarth following the death of Rhodri's brother in law, Gwgon.

During his reign, the Danes threatened the shores of Wales. They attacked Anglesey in 853 when they sacked the court of Aberffraw, killing inhabitants and looting before leaving the island in disarray. Three years later, Rhodri retaliated, defeating the Danes in battle near Llandudno.

Rhodri also had to deal with incursions by the Saxons on the borders, and it was here that he was killed in battle in 877.

Rhodri and his wife, Angharad, had six sons, two of them becoming the founders of royal lineages in Wales in the Middle Ages – Anarawd at Aberffraw, and Cadell, the father of Hywel Dda (the Good), at Dynefwr.

Rhodri's reign was important, as he displayed the strength which could exist when the whole country was united under one ruler.

Owain Gwynedd was born the first son of Gruffudd ap Cynan, in 1100. He had an older brother, Cadwaladr, with whom he worked while their father was alive, stabilising the hold Gruffudd had on Dyffryn Clwyd and some of the hundreds in Meirionnydd, Rhos and Rhufoniog, from the court at Aberffraw.

Owain Gwynedd reigned peacefully for several years after his father's death, building many castles to protect his Marcher lands.

In 1154 the King of England, Stephen, died and was followed by the ambitious Henry II, who invaded the northern Welsh borders with a view to taking Gwynedd. Although Henry did gain some land, Owain Gwynedd's army was particularly successful in harrassing Henry's troops through their guerilla 'sniping' tactics, and their knowledge of the hilly terrain, to the point when Henry lost patience and sought peace with the Welsh king. As a result, Owain promised a certain level of fealty to Henry, choosing to call himself Prince instead of King of Gwynedd. Owain was a diplomat as well as a soldier and it was largely due to his example that the native rulers of Wales came to take on the role of feudal magnates.

Owain died in 1170 and was buried at Bangor Cathedral. Llywelyn Fawr's exploits in medieval politics and on the battlefield earned him 20th century recognition when a plaque was unveiled to his memory at Llys Llywelyn in Aberffraw, the Anglesey Countryside Centre, in the area where he held court.

Llywelyn ap Iorwerth was born in the Conwy valley in 1173, but it is thought that he spent his youth in Powys where he was trained to be a soldier. Inter-family wrangling found him joining forces with his cousins against their uncle, Dafydd, when they snatched from him the greater part of mid Wales. Dafydd was trounced in battle again, near Aberconwy, and Llywelyn then added part of Gwynedd to his lands.

When he took Mold in 1197, Llywelyn became the only ruler in the northern part of Wales.

King John sought friendship with him and, as proof of his

sincerity, agreed to the marriage of his illegitimate daughter, Joan, with Llywelyn. But that friendship was short-lived. In 1210 John's army attacked Wales and Llywelyn lost mid Wales as a result, but regained it later.

He supported the English barons rebelling against the king, resulting in special dispensations for Wales being assured in Magna Carta, covering the re-possession of lost lands and rights, and the freedom to use Welsh law among the Welsh.

Llywelyn gradually gained more power over his co-princes and strengthened his position. Where it was necessary to keep the peace with his neighbours on the border, he did so by inter-marrying his and their children. When King John and the last of the princes died in 1215, this marked the stabilisation of Llywelyn's supremacy.

He resisted any attempt to bring the Welsh sees under the rule of Canterbury and used his influence to ensure that Welshmen were chosen to be bishops of St David's and Bangor in 1214. He supported the Cistercian order through the abbeys at Strata Florida, Aberconwy and Cymer, and founded an abbey at Llanfaes on Anglesey, where his wife was buried.

Llywelyn's dream was that Wales should become a feudal principality.

He died and was buried at the monastery at Aberconwy in 1240. When Edward I came to build his castles in North Wales, the monastery was demolished to make way for Conwy castle.

During Llywelyn's rule, Aberffraw was the chief seat of the Prince of Gwynedd, hence its choice for his memorial.

# Siôn Dafydd Rhys (1534-1619)

During the latter half of the 16th century a small group of educated Welshmen set out to try to modernise the Welsh Language and letters, codifying the language through compiling grammars and dictionaries.

Sion Dafydd Rhys was one of these Renaissance Welshmen. He was probably born in Llanfaethlu in 1534. A plaque to his memory is on the wall of The Coffee House in the village. He was the son of Dafydd Rhys, who was in service with Sir William Gruffudd at Llanfaethlu. It is possible that his father's roots were in south Wales, as he is said to have been in service with Lady Jane Stradling of St Donat's, who later became the wife of Sir William Gruffudd, so he could have travelled north with her.

Dafydd Rhys and his wife died while Sion Dafydd was small, and the boy was adopted by Sir John Stradling and educated at St Donat's.

He went up to Oxford at 18, to study for three years, but went down without a degree.

As was the fashion for young gentlemen whose families could afford it, Sion Dafydd Rhys travelled Europe, staying in Sienna in Italy where he studied physics. In 1562/3 he graduated M.D. His period at university there gave him the opportunity to learn Italian.

He taught for a while at a school in Pistoia while carrying on a medical practice, and while he was there wrote two books, one intended for Welshmen travelling the continent who were learning to speak Italian, and the other a Latin Grammar which was very popular with students.

By 1579 he had returned to Wales and there is evidence that he was headmaster at Friars School, Bangor for a short time from 1574. There is evidence that around 1583 he was in practice in Cardiff where he made friends among the gentry and re-forged his links with the Stradling family at St Donat's when Sir Edward Stradling became his chief patron.

He married Agnes, the daughter of John Garbet of Hereford. They moved to live at a house in Cwm Llwch at the foot of the Brecon Beacons. Here the couple had seven sons. Six died when young, and the remaining son became a priest in Brecon. Sion Dafydd Rhys's fame as a doctor spread to the borders and as far north as Gwynedd, from where patients would travel for his treatment. As his practice flourished, he also began to compile a Welsh Grammar, the main work of his life. It was written in Latin and dedicated to Sir Edward Stradling who very likely paid for its publication in 1592.

The book had a Latin introduction and a Welsh preface, and, plainly, was the result of detailed research. In it, Sion Dafydd Rhys gave excerpts of Italian poetry, comparing them with Welsh verse and noting similarities in poetic rules in both languages.

When he returned to Wales from Italy in the 1570s, Sion Dafydd Rhys took the Oath of Supremacy and became an active protestant. But there was insidious infiltration by missionary priests from the Roman Catholic seminaries into south Wales, and they succeded in reclaiming him to Catholicism.

As a secret adherent, he came under suspicion and in 1587 a posse of around twenty men raided his home to search for a Catholic printing press. Although their search proved fruitless, Rhys was arrested under suspicion, taken before the Council of the Marches at Ludlow, then to London to be examined by Archbishop Whitgift, the Archbishop of Canterbury. He was forced to take the Oath of Supremacy again before being freed and allowed to return home to Brecon.

For the remainder of his life he was careful not to appear to be a Catholic, although it was claimed that he was the author of a Catholic service book.

Agnes Rhys died in 1617, and her husband probably died in 1619 but his burial place is not known.

Professor Thomas Parry once commented, 'Everything considered, Rhys can be regarded as a characteristic example of the Renaissance Welshman'.

# Lewis Roberts (1596-1640)

A plaque in the entrance to Beaumaris Town Hall refers to 'Lewis Roberts – author'. One might be forgiven for thinking that he was a teller of tales, or a biographer, but perhaps a more true description would be 'Lewis Roberts – writer' as his expertise ran along certain more practical lines.

The 1954 Transactions of the Anglesey Antiquarian Society called him 'The first systematic writer on trade in the English language'.

Lewis Roberts was born in Beaumaris in 1596, the second son of Gabriel and Anne Roberts. Gabriel was an eminent merchant who bought his wares in Chester and had them shipped to Beaumaris, selling them from his warehouse there. In the late 16th century Beaumaris was an important port with several merchants operating from the town.

Gabriel Roberts amassed great wealth, and used it to buy land in Anglesey which eventually became the Castellior estate, lying between Pentraeth and what is now known as Four Crosses.

His children received an education, and Lewis went on to be employed by his father at the age of 13 'in the trade of merchandising'. When he was only 15 he was sent abroad, first to France where he was to learn as much as he could absorb at that age about trade, and to pick up as many languages as he could. Although he was to spend some time in France, Lewis Roberts remained anti-Catholic all his life.

He learnt to speak French while at Bordeaux, then proceeded to Rouen and Lyons in 1614/16 to study the money market.

He joined the East India Company in 1617, eventually

becoming a director, and spent time in Italy, Malaga and Tunis. While working in Constantinople as a factor he became connected with the Levant Company. During these years he constantly added to his knowledge of foreign trading and learnt several languages, becoming interested in the economies of the countries he visited.

He travelled Europe for twelve years, then came back to London and married the daughter of a London merchant.

Lewis Roberts was financially comfortable all his life. He was generous, presenting a collection of important early classical manuscripts to Jesus College library, Oxford, when he was working in Constantinople, to be followed by a collection of books in modern languages. Beaumaris Grammar School received a gift of books, too, and although he never returned to Anglesey to live, he held the island in high regard.

But Lewis Roberts is most well known for his 'Merchantes Mappe of Commerce', published in 1638. This contained fruits of his experience in foreign trading accumulated over the years, and was the first publication of its kind.

As was the fashion in publishing in the 17th century, the book bore a ponderous title. The front cover read 'The Merchantes Mappe of Commerce necessarie for all such as shall be employed in the public affaires of Princes in foraine partes; for all gentlemen and others that travell abroade for delight and pleasure; and for all Merchants or their factors that exercise the Art of Merchandising in any Parte of ye habitable world'.

The book contained maps, noted currencies and the chief commodities bought and sold in different countries throughout the world, weights and measures, all information vital to aspiring merchants who wished to expand their trade between London and cities abroad.

By 1700 the book had run to four editions and was regarded as the standard work of its kind. An appendix to the last edition also included a section on the advice of handling bills of exchange.

This treatise was introduced poetically, with contributions by

Izaac Walton who was a great friend, and by Lewis's young son, Gabriel, only nine years old at the time.

Izaac Walton wrote:

'If thou wouldst be a Gentleman, in more
Than one title onely, this Map yields thee store
Of Observation, fit for ornament
Or use, or to give curious cares content.

If thou wouldst be a Merchant: buy this book
For 'tis a prize worth gold; and doe not looke
Daily for such disbursements; no, 'tis rare
And should be cast up with thy richest ware.

Reader, if thou be any, or all three
(For these may meet and make a harmonie)
Then prayse this Author for his usefull paines
Whose aim is publike good, not private gains.'

Young Gabriel, the oldest of his four children, added

'A father's love may well excuse
The weakness of my infant muse
Yet, ('mongst the rest that praise thy pen)
At last admit mee say – Amen.'

In 1640 Lewis Roberts produced 'A Treasure of Trafficke' which outlined economic theory as it was regarded in his day, when it was believed that a country should regulate its trade by selling and buying through companies of merchants, and not through individual effort. Lewis was even in favour of some system of national insurance to this end. He was a man ahead of his time.

He died in London in 1640.

# Henry Rowlands (1655-1723)

One should hardly expect a book published in 1723 by an environmentalist-historian to be correct in every detail, bearing in mind the lack of scientific knowledge at the time it was written. But when published, Mona Antiqua Restaurata had a profound effect on what was to become a rising national interest in Wales in the country's heritage.

In the book, Henry Rowlands discusses Druidism and the ancient monuments in Anglesey. A second edition appeared in 1766.

The author was born in 1655 at Plas Gwyn, Llanedwen. Nothing is known about his early years, and it is thought he may have been educated at home, but when he was 27 years old he was ordained deacon at Bangor Cathedral and was given the living of Llanfair Pwllgwyngyll and Llantisilio in 1682. In 1696 he became vicar of Llanidan, Llanedwen, Llanddaniel-fab and Llanfair-y-cwmwd. He made his home at a house on the site of the present Plas Llwyn Onn, Llanidan, where he and his wife brought up twelve children.

Henry Rowlands had wide interests. He was an historian, a linguist and an amateur archaeologist. It was not only clerical and religious matters which filled his time. He was anxious that proper use should be made of the land. He studied the geography of Anglesey as well as its past history and archaeological remains. In fact nobody, until then, had researched Anglesey in as much detail as he had, and although his later critics accused him of displaying flights of fancy in his writing, all his readers have to admit that his work did contain interesting observations which deserved consideration.

Mona Antiqua Restaurata was his third published work. In 1704 he had produced an essay on agriculture in Anglesey. Founded on his own observations, this essay described the frequent use of sand and rotted seashells as fertilisers, and stressed the importance of providing shelter in the form of trees, walls and fences, for stock and crops.

This was followed in 1710 by a work on local antiquities called Antiquitates Parochiales, and discussed the parishes in his own commote of Menai.

Clearly, Henry Rowlands was influenced by his botanist friend, Edward Lhuyd, who was curator of the Ashmolean Museum in Oxford. Lhuyd had sent a questionnaire to many Welsh priests, begging local information on a number of topics including geography and natural history of their parishes. He intended to use the answers to the survey in a book.

As we have seen, Henry Rowlands had no less than five parishes in his care. Nevertheless he found time to provide the details requested about each, and one can imagine, being the man he was, how he was carried away by the interest those questions aroused. To Oxford went full details about the state of the land, crops and fertilisers; rivers and springs; the general appearance of the landscape and even a detailed description of the shore in his south-west corner of Anglesey, within the boundaries of his parishes. This research, done for a purpose other than his own, was to give him much food for thought, and material for his own writing.

Although some of the findings in his publications may be questioned today, his writings give a valuable insight into the ways of working of an early researcher, and are important for that fact alone.

Henry Rowlands was not a great traveller – he never visited England. But he found immense interest in, and was very knowledgeable about, his own neighbourhood. He died in 1723.

# William Jones (1674-1749)

The custom of a nobleman promoting the development of a tenant's child, one prevalent in the 17th century, was to prove the making of William Jones of Llanbabo.

William was born in 1674, the son of Sion Siors, a farmer at Y Merddyn, near Maenaddwyn at the foot of Bodafon mountain. Shortly after his birth, the family moved to Tyddyn Bach, Llanbabo, to farm land belonging to Lord Bulkeley. William attended the charity school at Llanfechell where his prowess with figures was soon recognised, and reached the ears of Lord Bulkeley who arranged for him to be apprenticed to a London merchant when it was time for him to leave school.

While working for the merchant, William was able to travel and he made a trip to the West Indies. He was successful in obtaining a teaching post on a man-of-war, where he taught mathematics and seamanship. His teaching methods were so remarkable and so successful that they came to the notice of Lord Anson, his naval officer, who recommended him to noble families needing a tutor for their children. Two of William's pupils were the Earl of Macclesfield and Philip Yorke, Earl Hardwicke. Both became Lord Chancellors of the realm.

The Earl of Macclesfield appointed William to teach his son at the family seat, Sherbourne Castle in Oxfordshire, where he remained living as a friend of the family once his tutoring post came to an end, with a sinecure salary of £200 per annum. This allowed him to continue mathematical research and writing in comparative comfort.

While at Sherbourne, William Jones lost most of his money through a bank foreclosure, but he surmounted his financial problems, thanks to friends.

When he was employed by the Earl of Macclesfield he was introduced to a London cabinet maker called Nix, a craftsman considered to be as important as Chippendale. He married Nix's daughter, Mary, in 1746.

During his life in London, William Jones wrote several books, among them A New Compendium of the whole art of navigation. In 1706 his second publication, Synopsis Palmarorium Mathesos (or a New Introduction to Mathematics) came to be considered the most important mathematics book of the day. William Jones was the first to set out rules governing compound interest, and he also wrote a number of books on higher mathematics.

By this time, calculus had been introduced, and in 1711, when the Royal Society appointed a committee to discuss differences of opinion on the subject, William Jones was a member. He was elected a Fellow of the Royal Society the following year, and later served as its deputy president.

The circles in which William Jones moved over the years explain why he became acquainted with many famous people. He was a friend of Halley and Izaac Newton and was given the task of editing some of Newton's scientific works. Dr Johnson was also an intimate friend, and introduced William to the Royal Society.

William and Mary Jones had three children, the youngest, another William, was destined to become an extremely proficient linguist, a solicitor, and finally he achieved his ambition to become a judge at the High Court at Calcutta, by virtue of which he received a knighthood.

William Jones the father died in July 1749, leaving behind what historian Angharad Llwyd recorded as 'a great reputation and moderate property'.

His collection of books, reputed to be the finest mathematical library in Britain, he left to the Earl of Macclesfield.

# William Bulkeley (1691-1760)

One of the unwitting contributors to our knowledge of 18th century life in Anglesey was William Bulkeley of Brynddu, Llanfechell.

Nobody knows why William began to keep a diary. He was 43 years old when he did so, and continued to the end of his life. Two of the three volumes remain safely housed in the University archives at Bangor. The other has been lost.

William wrote simply, as he would have spoken, about life as he saw it. He rarely, if ever, crossed the Menai Strait but lived the life of a not-too-affluent minor country squire. He was a member of the powerful Bulkeley family who had come to Anglesey many years before he was born, from Cheshire, but he had little contact with its head who lived at Baron Hill, Beaumaris.

His opinions about people, places and events were recorded fearlessly, with spirit, and often with a wry humour which makes his diaries so readable and enjoyable. No picture of William Bulkeley exists, but there is little need of any visual impression – his writing is sufficient. A visitor to Brynddu in 1760 says William stood thin-waisted to welcome him at the door, and sums him up as a kind and honest man.

When he was 19, William married Jane Lewis of Cemlyn and the couple had two children, Mary and William. Jane died on the birth of young William and her husband never quite recovered from the tragedy. He never contemplated re-marrying. From then on his life was spent looking after his affairs at home and in Ireland.

He was a landowner who farmed, shouldered responsibility,

*The tree-lined drive to Brynddu, home of William Bulkeley at Llanfechell.*

suffered financial reversals, and was constantly anxious about his children. He was a staunch supporter of the established church, but this did not prevent him from criticising roundly when he felt it necessary.

Relaxation came through reading the work of the Welsh poets. He would travel to Ireland occasionally, to see to his property and to visit a favourite cousin in Dublin.

The occasional political activity in Anglesey stirred up some heated opinions when he felt he had a responsibility to return a member to Westminster. One gains the impression that he would not be swayed by any fashionable argument. He was his own man.

William described himself as being 'among the class of the lesser Welsh gentlemen who had few financial resources and little inclination to toady to the English Court'. Some called William and his like 'the stay-at-home Welsh gentry'.

Brynddu, his home for so many years, stands a little way from the village square at Llanfechell, a solid stone house. Additions were made to the original building when Mary and the grandchildren went to live with him. The garden was his constant delight.

He bought trees in Dublin and had them shipped to Holyhead. One diary entry after an Irish visit mentions 'English elms, apple trees of different kinds, twelve yards of dwarf box for edging borders and currant trees for the walled garden'. He would spend hours botanizing – 'simpling' was the word he used – and brought home uncommon plants to grow in his orchard.

Although a landowner, William Bulkeley was not sufficiently wealthy to afford an agent and took hands-on responsibility for the farming activity. As now, the weather played an important part in the success or otherwise of his crops. He recorded the harvest of 1736 when he began to reap at the beginning of August as Llannerchymedd market prices were dropping. Thirteen of his farmhands took advantage of the sunshine on August 20 and he wrote in his diary: 'As usual at the end of my corn harvest, I praised God Almighty who gave seasonable weather for ripening the corn, and health to the inhabitance of the Island to get it in'.

Epidemics swept the country in the 18th century and they reached Anglesey. In 1740 the sickness was so great that William was forced to pay daily for ploughing as he did not know, from day to day, which men he could depend upon to arrive for work.

William Bulkeley had to serve his time as a member of the Grand Jury at the sessions in Beaumaris, and he would make the occasion a holiday, staying at a lodging house so that he could join his fellow jurors for conversation, drinking and dining with the judge, High Sheriff and Council. On April 28, 1734, he wrote 'I got up this morning at 8 o'clock, very much fatigued and sick after the Session's debauch'.

The greater part of these two volumes of William Bulkeley's diaries (we do not know the content of the missing one) relate his anxieties about his children.

Young William was a clerk to a lawyer in Chancery Lane, London, and his father sent him money regularly to see him through the Inns of Court. But young William did not reciprocate with any news about his progress. We read how his father had planned to marry him with one of the Lloyd daughters from Llwydiarth. As he put it, 'she was likely to come into her inheritance before long as her family were aged. This way my son would have been assured of a position in the county and my own finances might possibly have been restored'. Was the latter the ulterior motive? But fate and young William had other ideas and the arrangements came to nothing. Unfortunately son William took to drink and relations between him and his father deteriorated. He died at his uncle's home, Llys Dulas, in 1751.

William Bulkeley did not fare any better with his daughter. On a visit to her uncle in Dublin, Mary met Fortunatus Wright, a brewer and distiller from Liverpool, who seduced her. She married him in Dublin. The diary records how Fortunatus maltreated Mary over the years, resulting in several miscarriages. By 1748 there were two children living. William arranged schooling for them in Beaumaris, paying for it himself which created a drain on his finances. And he had to pay interest on loans raised by his son in law.

When war broke out between England and France, Fortunatus was involved in privateering, running a legitimate business in Italy to cover his tracks. He died at sea in 1757. William, ever ready to help his daughter, sent £50 to pay for her passage home. But her ship was wrecked off the Cornish coast and although she was saved she remained seriously ill at Penzance until October 1759 when William sent a man to Cornwall to bring her home.

'This in my 68th year,' he wrote in his diary. 'The financial burden of my daughter's unfortunate life cost me dear.'

But all was not misery. There were church activities (he was scathing about the sermons), games of football between parishes, and travelling plays, interspersed with visits to Ireland to enjoy some town life.

William Bulkeley's diary casts a bright light on 18th century Anglesey. He died in 1760 and is buried in the churchyard in Llanfechell.

*The grave yard at St Mechell's church, Llanfechell, where*
*William Bulkeley is buried.*

# The Morris Brothers (circa 1700)

Pentre Erianell, a farmhouse near Brynrefail, was the childhood home of the famous Morris brothers, Lewis, Richard, William and John. They were all talented in various ways. They were obsessional letter-writers and it is thanks to those letters, later collected and published in two volumes, that we have such a clear picture of life in Anglesey during the early 18th century. They wrote as freely as they would have conversed, on widely ranging topics from family to literature.

These four boys of Morris ap Rhisiart Morris and his wife Margaret were born at either Tyddyn Melys or Y Fferam near Bodafon, but the family moved over to the farm above Dulas bay in 1707.

John, the youngest, is the least well known. He went to sea where he became master's mate on the 'Torbay', a man-of-war, but was killed in a skirmish off the coast of Spain when he was 34 years old.

Richard left Anglesey for London when he was 15, and for some time had a hard life, when he was almost destitute. He was the least prolific of the letter-writers. Through the good offices of the Meyrick family of Bodorgan, whom his brother Lewis served for a while, he secured a clerical post with the Admiralty and eventually rose to chief clerk for foreign accounts to the Comptroller of the Navy. He married four times and fathered a tribe of children. Like his brother Lewis, Richard collected literary manuscripts and for a period oversaw the publishing of bibles at the S.P.C.K. through whom, in 1771, his edition of the Book of Common Prayer appeared, in large illustrated format.

*Wording on the plinth of the memorial to the Morris Brothers on a knoll close to their home at Pentre Erianell refers to their many, varied talents.*

Richard Morris's main claim to fame was as founder of the Cymmrodorion Society of which he remained President until his death in 1779. The Society still exists, and is noted for its scholarly lectures and publications.

Out of the 1000 letters sent by the Morris brothers, 400 were written by William, the second son,and 300 of them to Richard.

William spent most of his life in Holyhead, where he was a Comptroller of Customs. Like his brothers, he collected manuscripts and was an avid reader. Because of his sound common sense and business acumen, William was often called upon to give advice on legal and business matters. He was choirmaster at the parish church, and had a deep interest in church music. His chief interest, however, was his garden as he was a botanist of some note. Hugh Davies' 'Welsh Botanology' was said to have been based on William's knowledge.

William Morris died in 1763. According to his last letter in the collection, written to his brother Lewis, he was terminally ill himself when his father died, and was unable to attend the funeral.

The oldest of the Morris brothers, Lewis, is perhaps the most famous of the four. Although Lewis did not claim to have had much education, he had great ability. During his twenties, while living at Pentre Erianell, he was in business as a surveyor, working for local estates including that of the Meyrick family of Bodorgan.

In 1729 Lewis was appointed Inspector of Customs for Beaumaris and Holyhead, a post he held until 1743 on a part-time basis. Through the influence of the Bodorgan family and the Naval Office, he was commissioned in 1737 to survey some of the Welsh ports. Until then they had not been charted accurately. He began work in the summer of 1737, and for the next few years would spend the summer months roaming the coastline with his theodolite and way-wiser, and hiring a boat to go out to sea to measure depth. The winter was spent at home in Holyhead, converting the information he had collected into charts. Although this was commissioned work, he had few resources at his command, but produced astounding results. These included a chart of the coast of Wales from Gogarth (Llandudno) to Milford Haven, and an atlas, 'Plans of Harbours, Bars, Bays and Roads in St George's Channel including 25 detailed plans of Puffin Island and Black Point, Red Wharf Bay, Dulas Beach, Cemlyn, Holyhead, Malltraeth, Llanddwyn and Abermenai'.

These charts made the sailor's lot in coastal waters safer than in the past. They were published in 1748.

During the 1740's, Lewis left Anglesey for Cardiganshire where he had been appointed under-steward for Crown lands.

His Cardiganshire post involved overseeing mineral rights where lead mining was involved, and led to acrimony between local landowners and himself. They claimed what Lewis Morris declared to be an unfair share of the rich pickings. As he himself was also a shareholder in some of the mines, his opinions were hardly impartial. One such disagreement led to his being clapped in gaol for a period, and several times he was ordered to London to account for his stewardship.

Lewis Morris married twice. He went to live at his second wife's home at Penybryn, Goginan near Aberystwyth, where he died aged 65 in 1765 and was buried beneath the floor of Llanbadarn Church.

Contemporary writers give the impression that Lewis was a proud, scornful, moody man. But his good points far outweighed the criticisms. He supported literature and poetry. His interest in language prompted him to collect manuscripts, and by the middle of the 18th century he was acknowledged to be an expert on the Welsh language.

As a young man he had attempted to set up a Welsh press in Llannerchymedd, but the venture failed. He was more successful, briefly, with a similar press in Holyhead in 1735, when he published a small anthology of sixteen pages, Tlysau yr Hen Oesoedd (Gems of the Past) which was a collection of poetry and prose aimed at tempting Welsh readers who were turning more and more to English, to revert to reading in their own language. Only one issue appeared.

History and antiquities captured his attention, too, and he even compiled a dictionary of people and places entitled Celtic Remains. The manuscript is at the British Museum. Part was published in 1878, over a century after his death.

Other projects crowded Lewis Morris' fertile mind, but one lifetime was not long enough to see them come to fruition.

The Morris brothers were an astounding combination. They supported each other's interests, encouraging through their letters. Literary professor, W.J. Gruffydd, said of them:

'But for these three having thought their thoughts, worked at their tasks and lived as they did, it is certain that the 19th century would have been very different and Welsh literature today would have been far poorer.'

# Thomas Ellis (1711/12-1792)

The connection with Jesus College, Oxford and Thomas Ellis, one of its scholars from Flintshire, was to bring him to Holyhead where his stay was to have an influence upon life in the town.

Thomas Ellis was born in Galltmelyd and went up to Jesus College when he was 16 years old. He first graduated in 1731 and added a Divinity degree in 1741. He was a Fellow of the college from 1731-1761.

In 1737 the lectureship (to say services and to preach) at Holyhead was assigned to him, and he quickly made his presence felt in the town, where he was later termed rector.

Thomas Ellis proved to be a busy clergyman who demonstrated Puritanical strictness. He was interested in education and although an Anglican he supported nonconformist Griffith Jones and his circulating schools, and was one of only half a dozen clergymen in Wales appointed by Griffith Jones to receive contributions to the movement.

One of Thomas Ellis' parishioners at St Cybi's church was William Morris, one of the famous Morris brothers of Pentre Erianell. His garden and that of Thomas Ellis shared a boundary. On the recommendation of Morris, Thomas was admitted to the Cymmrodorion Society of which he became a corresponding member.

As a clergyman and someone eager to support Welsh literature and publications in Welsh, Thomas Ellis was one of those who, in 1746, facilitated the printing of the Welsh bible by the S.P.C.K., also supported by William Morris' brother Richard in London.

Thomas Ellis had what he termed 'real concern for ye swarm

of children, which grow in a manner wild for want of schooling'. So he began a free school for the poor children of Holyhead, for which he was for ever begging money from whoever he thought had money to spare for the cause.

Thomas Ellis wrote letters, and as many of those letters are still in safe keeping today we can gain a picture from reading them of social conditions in Holyhead in the 18th century.

He was familiar with the Owen family of Penrhos, the estate on the edge of the town, and when Hugh Owen was an invalid at Bristol he kept in constant touch with him, giving him news of home and particularly of the birth of Hugh's daughter, Margaret, which took place in his absence and whom he was never to see.

Thomas Ellis' description of the baptism of Margaret 'the little Miss – as pretty a young lady as ever one would desire to toast' and her mother, as 'brave and jolly' was graphic and, at the same time, touched with pathos.

The school that Thomas Ellis founded was held in the tiny chapel which stands at the entrance to the graveyard at St Cybi's, once called Capel y Bedd (The Chapel of the Grave) and remained there until 1817 when the National School was built. Capel y Bedd then reverted to church use, and is still used as a church room. The present school still carries Thomas Ellis' name.

As part of his ministry in Holyhead, he carried out a cleaning-up process of morals, stressing the sanctity of Sunday and persuading the youth of the town to hold their local saint's day celebrations on a weekday instead of Sunday. He was outwardly antagonistic against Methodism and in 1747 published a tract against the movement. Doubtless his parishioners were warned of consorting, and showing sympathy with the Wesleys.

'There are about six Methodists in this parish,' he wrote, 'but their behaviour is mended of late and they all attend the church constantly except the teacher, one Owen David a cooper that lives near the town who has often broken his engagements with me.'

By 1759 it was time for Thomas Ellis to move on, and Jesus College gave him its most valuable living, at Nutfield in Surrey, where he received a considerably greater stipend, so allowing him to marry in 1762. He brought up two children. He died at Nutfield in 1792, aged 80.

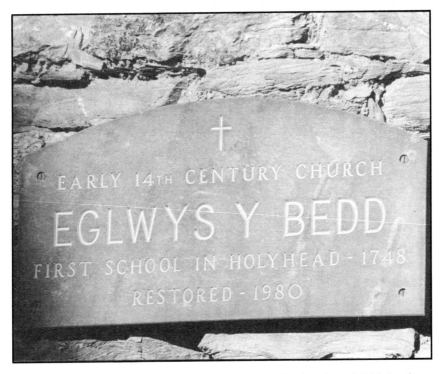

*Thomas Ellis's school at Eglwys y Bedd, St Cybi's churchyard, Holyhead, is remembered by a commemorative plaque on the outer wall.*

# Goronwy Owen (1723-1769)

One of Wales' foremost 18th century Renaissance poets was born at Rhosfawr, Brynteg, in the parish of Llanfair Mathafarn Eithaf in 1723, the son of an itinerant tinker who travelled around the countryside mending dishes, jugs and drinking vessels wherever there was a need.

Goronwy's mother, to whom he was close throughout her life, wanted better things for her son, and saw to it that he received schooling at Llanallgo and later at Friars School, Bangor, where he began to learn Latin.

At Friars School, Goronwy began to read and write poetry, too, an obsession which was to remain with him throughout his life, and cushion his hardships by offering an outlet for his creativity.

When he was 18, his mother approached Owen Meyrick of Bodorgan to see if he could offer the means of a scholarship at Jesus College, Oxford, as she had dreams of her son entering the church. In 1742 Goronwy was admitted to Jesus College as a servitor, but shortly afterwards his mother died. This was a great loss to him and his enthusiasm for learning disappeared. He left Oxford and returned home, but did not receive a warm welcome from his father, so obtained an assistant teacher's post at the free school in Pwllheli. This was followed by a similar post in Denbigh where he taught Latin in exchange for bed and board.

Goronwy Owen was ordained deacon at Bangor Cathedral in 1746 when he returned to Llanfair Mathafarn Eithaf to occupy a curacy for a short time before being forced to give way to a higher class candidate, and going to the church in Selattyn, near

Oswestry, where he spent two and a half years.

Here, Goronwy Owen was ordained priest, and married.

Throughout his life, he was discontented with his work and longed to return to Wales. But circumstances were to take him even farther away.

While in Selattyn he was arrested and accused of debt. His trial was followed by a prison sentence in Shrewsbury. When he was freed, his church did not welcome his return, so he moved to Uppington to take a teaching post at Donnington Grammar School, living in the school house for four and a half years, farming six acres and looking after parish affairs. And he wrote poetry. He wrote a poem every month and sent it to his friend, Lewis Morris, for criticism.

A period of curacy at Walton, Liverpool, followed. His daughter was born here (he already had two sons) but she died when she was eighteen months old.

When teaching at Walton, a contemporary wrote of Goronwy Owen 'he was a smart little active man . . . was fond of the exercise of walking and he always carried a long overhand walking stick . . . he had no objection to a Cheerfull Glass, but was oppressed with a numerous Family'.

To put the tragedy of his daughter's death behind them, the family moved to London, Goronwy hoping that the Cymmrodorion Society members there might find him work as a translator and pay him for 'priesting in Welsh' in a chapel or church on a Sunday. Although his friends among the London Welsh were kind to him, this did not happen and he lived on charity for a time before being offered the living of Northolt in Middlesex. He stayed here for two years, and this is where he wrote his most famous poem, a song of longing for his native land. Once again, he had financial difficulties – a clergyman's pay was minimal – and decided to try his fortune in a completely new environment.

A lectureship at the College of William and Mary in Williamsburg in America attracted him – or perhaps it was the stipend of £200 a year – so in 1757 the family sailed from

England. The voyage was uncomfortable, there was a great deal of sickness, and Goronwy's wife and one son died before they reached land.

To add to his difficulties, the college staff offered only a chilly welcome, as they objected to someone from England being appointed in favour of an American. For a time Goronwy appeared to have surmounted the problem and made himself acceptable, even to the point of marrying the sister of the college principal. Again, tragedy struck. His wife died soon after the marriage. Goronwy slipped back to his old ways and was charged with being slipshod in his work and drunk, and he had to resign.

His brother-in-law found a living for him, and he moved once more, to become priest of St Andrews, Brunswick County.

This was a huge parish, as big as Anglesey, but sparsely populated. Here Goronwy Owen spent nine years. He bought 400 acres of land, and the slaves to work it, and grew tobacco. He built himself a house and married for a third time. He appeared to have settled, but was still homesick and complained because he heard no Welsh spoken.

His troublesome life came to an abrupt end in 1769 when he died and was buried on his plantation.

Goronwy's life had been troubled since his mother died. He had personal problems and suffered poverty. He wrote no fewer than 78 letters to the Morris Brothers, many of them from America, in which he told how he longed for Welsh books and manuscripts. His ambition to write an epic poem, similar to Milton's 'Paradise Lost', came to nothing. But he did leave some treasures which today's critics regard as superb pieces of poetry.

His will and inventory are preserved in the Will Books of Brunswick. His home, called the Goronwy Owen House, stands on the banks of Reedy Creek at Dolphin, north of Lawrenceville, and is now open as a small museum in his memory.

# Thomas Williams (1737-1802)

Above Beaumaris stands Cefn Coch, the farmhouse which was the birthplace of Thomas Williams who is remembered by a plaque on the old Llansadwrn school.

The story goes that Thomas' father, Owen Williams, was ploughing at Cefn Coch when his ploughshare struck a solid object which was found to be a kettle, full of gold. Fact or fiction? No matter, but the truth is that Owen Williams did obtain a fortune in some way, which allowed him to educate his son and later to buy the nearby estates of Treffos at Llansadwrn and Tregarnedd at Llangefni.

Thomas, after being articled to a solicitor in Denbigh, went as assistant to a lawyer in Beaumaris. His family connections and his ability led to his becoming steward to Lord Boston from whom he leased Llanidan Hall, Brynsiencyn. While living there he improved both hall and farm.

During his practising years as a lawyer, he was instrumental in sorting out many legal problems among the more wealthy landowners in Anglesey, acting as land and estate agent for them, and his reputation grew apace.

A vein of copper had been discovered on Mynydd Parys, Amlwch, and the Lewis family of Llys Dulas called in Thomas Williams to sort out their boundary claim to part of the mountain, against that of Nicholas Bayly of Plas Newydd for his section at Cerrig y Bleiddia, and to ensure that ores mined were worked separately.

It was not only the legalities of the project which appealed to him. He became involved in the business also when, in 1778, he joined with the Rev. Edward Hughes who had married into the

Lewis family, and John Dawes, a London banker, to form The Parys Mine Company, which was to employ eight hundred workers.

In 1785 he gained greater responsibility for the Parys Mountain mining project by forming a second company, Mona Mine Company, through collaborating with the Plas Newydd family, which also gave him control of the working of Cerrig y Bleiddia on the eastern side, and therefore the whole area of the mountain. Considerable money was invested in the mines, which proved to have been a wise move as profits soared.

These two companies became one of the greatest industrial projects of the 18th century. Thomas Williams was involved with all aspects, as business manager for both.

Copper made Thomas Williams a wealthy man. He dominated the industry in Britain, building his own smelting works at Amlwch, Ravenhead in Lancashire, and Swansea, and brass and copper works at Holywell, in South Wales and in the Thames Valley. Offices and stores were located in Liverpool, and he had commercial ventures in Chester, Bangor and Caernarfon.

At one time, a fleet of forty ships plied regularly from Amlwch to Holywell, carrying copper ore for smelting.

The Cornish copper industry was also taken over by him. For five years he was responsible for selling all Cornish copper. In 1799 he was called before the House of Commons to testify to the state of the copper industry in Britain.

The success of the industry was given impetus by the decision of the Navy to copper-bottom all their wooden ships, following losses during the American War of Independence. Copper bolts replaced iron bolts for fastening sheathing, a change which created great demand and so strengthened the market.

Other countries followed suit, with the result that Britain exported to France, Spain and Holland. Thomas Williams also arranged profitable contracts with the East India Company, and with the African trade.

By 1800 it was claimed that half the copper market was in the hands of Thomas Williams, to the tune of around a million pounds.

As well as being an international industrial figure, Thomas Williams was a benefactor to Anglesey. Known locally as 'Twm Chwarae Teg' (Tom Fair Play), he was regarded as a genial, magnanimous character, quick to see a possibility for improvement and even quicker to act upon it. He contributed generously to the £4,000 needed for the new church at Amlwch in 1800. He farmed his Anglesey lands wisely. For example, he was the first to grow swedes on the island, which proved to be a better crop for the farmer as they could be stored for longer than the small turnips which farmers had been growing in the past.

When Thomas Williams died at Bath in 1802, he owned five mansions and his estate was worth half a million pounds, a vast sum in those days.

He had served for a number of years as Member of Parliament for Great Malvern.

His remains were brought to Llanidan Churchyard for burial, and thirty years later disinterred, with those of his family, and re-buried in Llandegfan churchyard.

Thomas Williams, as so often happens to those in high places, made enemies in his own industry, but after his death one obituary to him read 'Take him all in all, it is hardly to be expected that we shall meet his like again'.

William Bingley, writing of his own travels in Anglesey, called Parys Mountain 'that inexhaustible mine of copper'. But the success of copper mining at Parys Mountain declined after Thomas Williams' death as the ore was becoming increasingly difficult to extract, and his forceful character was no longer behind the industry.

# Hugh Davies (1739-1821)

Botanists the world over, and Anglesey botanists in particular, are indebted to Hugh Davies, the son of a Llandyfrydog vicar, for his careful research into the flora of Anglesey in the 18th century, resulting in his famous 'Welsh Botanology – a systematic catalogue of the native plants of Anglesey in Latin, English and Welsh' of 1813.

He was born in Llandyfrydog in 1739, one of several children of Lewis Davies and his wife, Mary. His father died when Hugh was 10 years old, and his mother entered him as a scholar at the Beaumaris Free Grammar School. From there he went to Jesus College, Oxford, where he graduated B.A., in 1762 and M.A., in 1768.

He was ordained deacon while he was still at Oxford, and priest by the Bishop of Bangor in 1764.

In 1763, he returned to Anglesey as curate to Llangefni with Tregaian.

In 1774 Hugh Davies visited the Isle of Man along with Thomas Pennant, who paid tribute to him as a botanist by writing 'To him we owe the account of our Snowdonia plants. To him I lie under the obligation that in June 1775 at my request he undertook another voyage to the Isle of Man to take a second review of its vegetable production. By his labours a Flora of the Island is rendered as complete as it is possible to be effected by a single person in one season of the year. The number of Plants he observed amounted to 550'.

Hugh Davies' all-consuming interest in natural history was to mean a corresponding disinterest in his calling. Those were the days when it was possible to accept a curacy and, if one had the means, to pay someone else to carry out parish duties in one's absences, which could be protracted. Hugh Davies filled several curacies in this way, and when he was eventually put in charge of Abergwyngregyn as rector, he had no fewer than six curates during his 29 years there.

He assisted Thomas Pennant with his 'India Zoology' published in 1790 by editing the greater part of the work.

In 1790, too, he was elected a Fellow of the Linnean Society and he assisted other noted botanists and naturalists in the publication of their works.

From his many letters, now safely deposited at the National Library of Wales, one surmises that Hugh Davies must have been hypochondriacal as there are many written to a doctor friend about his medical complaints – perhaps these were slightly exaggerated especially at the time when, as rector of Abergwyngregyn, he was absent from his duties for two years but still succeeded in making journeys to study plants and continue with his letter-writing and the work on his Flora.

Hugh Davies' 'Welsh Botanology' catalogued over eight hundred species of plants as well as the mosses and lichens he saw in Anglesey. He divided them into their various classes, adding the Latin, English and Welsh names, and noted where they could be found.

In his introduction he said he had three aims. He wanted to note where the plants grew; he tried to reason why they could be found there, and then added facts which would be of interest to those living in, and visiting, Anglesey.

Today's botanists can follow in his footsteps across the island and still find the plants which Hugh Davies saw over two centuries ago.

He died in 1821, in his 82nd year, and was buried in Beaumaris churchyard. There is a mural tablet to his memory in Beaumaris church.

# Christmas Evans (1766-1838)

Not all Anglesey's worthies have been born and bred on the island. Christmas Evans, Baptist minister and one of Wales' most famous preachers, is a case in point.

He was born in Esgairwen, Llandysul in Ceredigion, the son of a cobbler. As a parish apprentice, he was sent to work as a labourer on local farms. One of these farms, Castell Hywel, belonged to David Davis who also ran a school. Under Davis' influence, young Christmas Evans joined the church and learned to read Welsh, English and a smattering of Latin.

At 21 he joined the Baptist church in Aberduar where the atmosphere was not so staid, and suited his temperament. In this revivalist setting he listened to travelling preachers and, full of zeal for the cause, accepted the invitation to return to Llŷn with them to preach to the Baptists of the peninsula.

By this time his preaching ability had been honed to suit his listeners. He understood the people, and what they expected and appreciated from their preachers. He realised how he could use drama to project his message. He was becoming known in Baptist circles.

In 1789 Christmas Evans was ordained, and in the same year he married Catrin Jones.

The Baptists had two chapels in Anglesey, at Cildwrn outside Llangefni, and Capel Newydd at Mynydd Parys. Other congregations on the island met in private houses. The Revd Seth Morris had responsibility for all the Anglesey Baptists but, when a visiting preacher, the Revd Thomas Morris, made an impression and some of the congregations wanted him to be their minister, ill-feeling grew.

In 1786 the congregations divided, five under the wing of one minister and four under the other. They remained divided in this way until 1801, when they settled their differences as Thomas Morris left Anglesey and Seth Morris was no longer at Llangefni. United again, the Anglesey Baptists invited Revd Christmas Evans to minister to all.

When he arrived in Anglesey, he met with a certain amount of opposition due to feelings aroused by the previous divisions, and also the infiltration of the new doctrine of Sandemanism. This was an extreme sect, a religious party expelled from the Church of Scotland for maintaining that national churches, being 'kingdoms of this world', were unlawful. It was formed by a break-away member, Robert Sandeman.

But the strong, revivalist preaching of Christmas Evans, which appealed to the people, soon swept away any discord and his popularity grew. Within two years, the number of Baptist churches on the island had increased.

Christmas Evans was dogmatic, a leader who liked to think of himself as 'The Bishop of Anglesey'. Such was his influence within his own denomination not only in Anglesey but throughout Wales that other Baptist ministers were referred to slyly, by other denominations, as 'Christmas' chickens'.

He made tours of South Wales twice a year, preaching at the more affluent churches to raise funds for the Baptist cause. An arresting figure physically – he had only one eye – and with a commanding personality and voice, he was in demand for preaching meetings and special occasions.

But having such a strong personality could make for problems, and all was not plain sailing in Anglesey when one of the churches chose a minister contrary to the wishes of Christmas Evans. Some even refused to contribute their share towards his own upkeep.

His popularity on the island began to wane. His wife Catrin died and he was a lonely man, and near destitute. He therefore moved in 1826 to Caerffili in South Wales. Later he took the responsibility of churches in Cardiff and Caernarfon

Christmas Evans spoke out for the Welsh Baptists in many theological discussions of his day. He was generous with the little money he had – he gave £1 a year to the Bible Society and half a sovereign to the Baptist Mission when his own salary was only £17 a year, and counted himself morally responsible for the debts of the churches in his care.

His most famous sermons were delivered very much in the manner of dramatic presentations, and they had a great influence on his congregations.

He died on a visit to Swansea in 1838, and is buried close to Bethesda chapel where he was to have preached.

# Henry William Paget,
# 1st Marquess of Anglesey (1768-1854)

As the visitor to Anglesey crosses the Menai Strait by the Britannia Bridge, the great monument to Henry William Paget soars above the road.

Paget was born in London and educated at Westminster School and at Oxford. In 1790 he was elected Member of Parliament for Arfon boroughs, and represented that constituency (or another at Milborne Port) for periods between 1790 and 1812, when he succeeded his father in the House of Lords as Lord Uxbridge.

He was first and foremost a soldier and in 1793 he raised his own company. During the fighting in Flanders in 1794-5 he led a brigade of foot soldiers. Then in 1797 he was given the command of the 7th Light Dragoons and remained their commanding officer for forty-five years.

Visitors to his Anglesey home, Plas Newydd, can see relics of the battle for which he gained most fame, Waterloo, where he served under Wellington and lost a leg as a result of the battle, when a stray shot caught his right knee, and amputation was necessary. He was honoured with the title Marquess of Anglesey by George IV for the part he played on the battlefield.

When Wellington became prime minister, the Marquess was chosen to be Lord Lieutenant of Ireland. He reached Dublin during demands that the Catholics should be given the vote, and soon realised that an uprising would occur should the vote not be given. Neither the King nor Wellington agreed, and the Marquess was recalled. This strained relations between Paget and the Duke, but their friendship was cemented again in their later years. The Marquess returned to Ireland in 1830 but resigned in 1833 because of ill health, and died the following year.

He married twice, the first time with Lady Caroline Villiers by whom he had eight children. In 1809 he left her for Lady Charlotte Wellesley, Wellington's sister in law. He divorced Caroline, and married Lady Charlotte. There were ten children from the second marriage.

The 1st Marquess of Anglesey was considered a dandy, and was one of George IV's close friends. He was a rich man, benefitting from the copper mine at Mynydd Parys to the tune of over £75,000 a year.

At Plas Newydd the Waterloo Room displays his uniforms, and one of the first articulated artificial limbs ever made, a leather and wooden leg which he wore following his amputation.

After Waterloo and the conferring of the title, the local people of Caernarfon and Anglesey collected towards erecting the stone column in his honour. It was not until six years after his death that the 3.5 metre bronze statue of the Marquess was added.

*The first Marquess of Anglesey looks out across the Menai Strait
from his commemorative column.*

# Richard Evans (1772-1851)

To appreciate the contribution made by Richard Evans to Anglesey life, one needs to know some of his family history.

One stormy night in 1745, a smuggler named Dannie Lukie was sailing towards the Skerries off the north coast of Anglesey when he came upon a ship in difficulties and about to sink in the mountainous seas. Although the waves were huge and the night was dark, he managed to make out three figures in a boat which had cast off from the sinking ship, a man and two boys. At great risk to himself the smuggler eventually reached the boat, only to find that the man had died, but the two terrified boys were still alive. He took them ashore to Mynachdy, a country house nearby, where they were cared for until they recovered.

It is not known what happened to one, but the other was adopted by the owner of Mynachdy, Dr Lloyd, who believed him to be Spanish. The boy was given the name Evan Thomas.

Evan spent his early years doing jobs about the farm, but Dr Lloyd soon noticed that the youngster had a special ability – he could mend broken bones. This gift first came to light when he mended a chicken's leg. As the boy grew older his gift was even more evident, and Dr Lloyd would take him on his rounds whenever there was likely to be need for bone-setting. For his part, Evan learned about surgery as he accompanied the doctor.

Eventually Evan Thomas married and had four sons. Richard was the third and he, too, possessed the gift of bone-setting.

Richard was born in 1772, probably at Maes y Merddyn Brych, Llanfairynghornwy. Early in his life he was known as Richard ap Evan Thomas (son of Evan Thomas) which became shortened to Richard Evans.

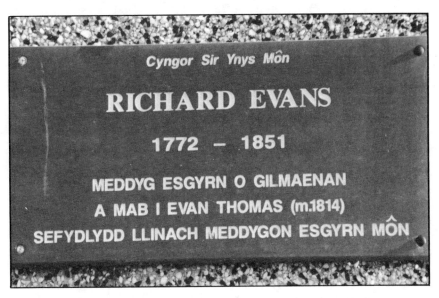

*The plaque at Cilmaenan cites Richard Evans as 'bonesetter of Cilmaenan, and son of Evan Thomas (d. 1814) the founder of the Anglesey bone-setting dynasty'.*

*Cilmaenan, Llanfaethlu, the farmhouse home of Richard Evans, bone-setter.*

He married Margaret Jones from a farm called Bodfardden Wen in a ceremony called 'priodas cefn ceffyl' (horseback wedding), where the couple and their guests rode on horseback from her home to Llanfaethlu where they were to live at Cilmaenan, a farm on the road down from Llanfaethlu to Porth Swtan (Church Bay).

Richard Evans was described as conscientious, austere, deeply religious, well read, he attended the Methodist chapel in Llanfaethlu. Such was his fame, he was called upon to set broken bones over a wide area of Anglesey, although farming was his chief occupation. He was even requested by Lord Stanley to attend one of his sons at Alderley in Cheshire.

He was a proud man, to whom social status meant little. The story goes that he was called upon to treat a traveller at Gwyndy, the coaching inn between Bodffordd and Bodedern, who had suffered an accident on his way. Richard Evans arrived so roughly dressed, presumably in his working clothes, that the patient would not receive him, so Richard returned home, his journey wasted. The innkeeper persuaded the patient to change his mind and Richard Evans was sent for a second time. But he refused to make the journey again.

When he died, in 1851 at 79 years of age, Richard Evans left twenty-seven grandchildren.

The gift of mending broken bones was passed on to other members of the family, but Richard Evans is the one remembered on the plaque on the wall of his old home, Cilmaenan.

# Owen Williams (1774-1859)

A plaque at Llannerchymedd school to Owen Williams refers to him tersely as 'musician'.

Owen Williams contributed extensively to Welsh congregational singing of his period, as he sought to advise teachers how to transmit knowledge to pupils of all ages.

His first book, published in 1817, was called Egwyddor-Ddysg, neu Catecism ar Reolau Cerddoriaeth and was a Welsh translation of an essay on the work of Charles Dibdin.

His second book, Egwyddorion Canu (The Rudiments of Singing) advised how to teach Welsh voices to sing religious music more correctly. The two books were published in one volume in 1818 and became popular throughout Wales.

It was followed in 1819 by a collection of hymn tunes in two volumes, the first consisting of music for the psalms of Edmwnd Prys and the second intended for the new measures being introduced by William Williams, Pantycelyn, and the more modern hymn-writers. Most of the music, he claimed, was a collection of Welsh melodies not hitherto published, but there were also one or two tunes and melodies by Handel, Purcell and Arne adapted for hymn singing. There were 273 psalm tunes and hymns in the collection.

The second book contained old melodies, and some modern ones not published before.

Sponsors for this collection included the Queen, the royal family, archbishops and bishops and other famous people of the day.

One local sponsor was Lewis Ellis of Beaumaris, named 'organ builder', who built himself an organ for his home, Pen

Twr, Henblas, in Anglesey in 1787 and in 1790 installed it in Beaumaris church.

In the course of his life, Owen Williams travelled widely to lecture on music, and this had an added advantage as he could collect tunes as he did so.

His fourth book was published in 1827 – 'The Harp of David King of Israel, or Royal Psalms of Zion'. Owen Williams lost a lot of money on this publication, and it left him a poor man. It was only through the influence of the Hon. Charles Watkin Williams Wyn that he was given a post as hall porter at His Majesty's Stamp and Tax Office in 1827 that his financial position improved.

It is not known where he died, or where he was buried.

*The plaque at Llannerchymedd school to Owen Williams,*
*'pioneer of congregational singing'.*

# John Elias (1774-1841)

'The preacher with the pointed finger' is how Welsh Calvinistic Methodists of the early 19th century remembered John Elias.

He was a gifted orator, had a virile imagination, and his good looks and powerful voice made an instant impression on early 19th century congregations who were swayed by his ardour.

He was born in 1774 at Brynllwyn Bach, Abererch near Pwllheli, the son of weaver. His early religious training came from his grandfather, who he admired so much that he adopted his name and made it his own surname.

John Elias went, for a short time, to Evan Richardson's school in Caernarfon. He was ordained by the Calvinistic Methodist church in 1811 and, shortly after, married Elizabeth Broadhead of Tre'r Gof, Llanbadrig.

Elizabeth came from a well-known Anglesey family. Her father and mother were Anglicans and did not look favourably on her marriage, so prior to the wedding she left home and went to stay with an aunt and uncle near Llanfflewin. The nonconformists were not happy about her liaison either. When she went to hear John Elias preach, she was advised 'If you join us, Miss Broadhead, you must leave off wearing that lace collar'.

The couple went to live in Llanfechell, where Elizabeth kept a grocer's shop and looked after the children, so freeing John to continue his evangelising. By dint of hard work she managed to finance schooling for the two remaining children of the marriage – two had died young.

The marriage was not to last, however. Elizabeth was lost at sea during a voyage of the 'Marchioness of Anglesey' sailing from Liverpool to Amlwch in April 1818, when the ship

*John Elias's tomb at Llanfaes*

foundered at Llys Dulas and all but three of the passengers and crew were drowned.

Two years later, John Elias married the widow of Sir John Bulkeley, Presaeddfed, and the couple went to live at Fron, Llangefni.

John Elias was a spirited campaigner for what he believed was right, and a fearless antagonist where loose morals were in question. He was the most popular preacher of his day in Wales. Through his preaching he overturned many hitherto popular but unsavoury activities, such as any desecration of the Sabbath which included holding hiring fairs, drinking, and scavenging for jetsam along the shores where ships had been driven on the rocks or sunk.

He was a Tory, voting against the Reform Bill of 1832. He called for better training for ministers, and he was a keen supporter of the Bible Society.

John Elias died from gangrene of the foot. Like most events during his life, his funeral was considered especially newsworthy. He died in Liverpool, but plans were made for him to be buried in the churchyard at Llanfaes. Work stopped locally on the day of the funeral, shops closed, curtains were drawn. Vessels at Beaumaris flew their flags at half mast. Walking in front of the hearse were the four doctors who had attended him. By the time the cortege reached Porthaethwy, forty-one coaches and one hundred and eighty-four men on horseback had joined the procession along with nearly all the ministers from Anglesey chapels.

The chapel in Llangefni with which he was associated was demolished some years ago, but there is a plaque to his memory in the Moriah Chapel on Glanhwfa Road.

# Robert Roberts (1777-1836)

John Robert Lewis (1731-1806) was a Holyhead author, hymn writer and publisher and, as a young man, had been interested in astronomy. He opened a school around 1760. The books he published reflected his interests – religion and mathematics – but he is better remembered for publishing the first Welsh almanac in 1761.

Almanacs were popular. They consisted of a year's calendar with other useful information such as the dates of fairs, tide tables, times of sunrise and sunset. The Holyhead almanacs of John Robert Lewis were published without a break for forty-four years.

John Robert Lewis and his wife, Margaret, had six children, Robert being the first born. Robert (who dropped his surname in favour of Roberts) was given a good education, although little else is known about his early years except that he was a frequent visitor to London. It was while he was attending The Burlington Academy that his father died. At the age of 18, young Robert returned home to be head of the family, and to carry on the family business of which publishing the annual almanac was part.

In 1807 he, like his father before him, opened a school which remained at Mill Street, Holyhead, until 1835. His brother joined him as teacher.

The Mill Street curriculum was extensive. Pupils were offered arithmetic, reading and writing, book-keeping, science, and Latin and English Grammar. Also taught was 'Geometry (plain and spheric trigonometry applied to the theory and practice of mensuration in general such as surveying of land, coasts, harbours, lengths and distances, artificer's work etc., the construction of maps and charts). Also navigation including the mode of ascertaining the longitude by lunar observation.'

While running the Mill Street school, Robert carried on the publishing business.

The almanacs were printed at Trefriw in the Conwy valley by John Jones. They carried the fake publisher's imprint, 'Dublin', to avoid paying government tax. Although the practice was illegal, this enabled Robert to sell at a lower price, so more copies could be sold. The tax, the crippling Stamp Duty, came to an end in 1833.

Robert Roberts married Mary Owen of Holyhead. He had a wide variety of interests apart from his business, and their listing makes one wonder how he fitted all in to a lifespan.

As a geographer, he published several maps. The telescope he had installed in the upper storey of his home had two purposes – for scanning the night sky, and for picking up semaphore signals from ships beyond the harbour, for the Irish packet service.

He played the organ at St Cybi's church, was church warden, and was particularly knowledgeable about church music. He made a new sundial for the church when the building was refurbished. He owned property in Holyhead, and was interested in agriculture.

For a time, Robert acted as estate manager to the Penrhos estate, meeting people of note in the course of his duties. Everything happening in Holyhead was of interest to him.

Robert Roberts began to publish his own magazine for Anglesey, Eurgrawn Môn (literally translated, golden grain of Anglesey) of which twenty-one issues appeared before it ceased. This was, in all probability, the first Welsh 'county' magazine.

His most important publications, however, reflected his scientific interests. They were Daearyddiaeth Gymreig (Welsh Geography) and Seryddiaeth neu lyfr gwybodaeth yn dangos rheoliad y planedau ar berson dynion (Astronomy, or an

*The Holyhead almanacists, John Robert Lewis and his son, Robert Roberts, share the memorial on the stair wall at Holyhead Library.*

informative book showing how the planets govern man).

The first part of Daearyddiaeth Gymreig left the press in 1812, and not without a great deal of anxiety. Selling books in the 19th century was a risky business, and sponsors had to be found before publication could be contemplated. In preparing the manuscript, Robert had the advice of three experts. They were writer and antiquarian John William Pritchard of Plas y Brain, Llanbedrgoch; Paul Panton of Plas Gwyn, Pentraeth, barrister and antiquarian; and grammarian, editor and antiquarian William Owen Pughe, a London-based Welshman. All gave advice, and much of it was incorporated in the final manuscript. But it all entailed frequent editing, re-writing and re-designing.

Robert drew the maps himself, sending them to London for the plates to be made. He was probably the first cartographer to publish maps in Welsh.

After struggling for four years to see the effort successfully concluded, copies reached Holyhead in 1816. A gazeteer appeared later. This, and other works published by Robert Roberts, left him heavily in debt.

His first wife died in 1832, and he married again in the following year.

He applied for a licence to set up a printing press in Bryngwran, and was successful, but he died shortly after, in 1836 when he was 58 years old. The plaque commemorating his life and work is at Holyhead Library.

# James Williams (1790-1872) and Frances Williams (1797-1858)

The Anglesey coastline, glorious on a calm summer's day, is a perilous place in a storm. The seas off shore are littered with the wrecks of small ships and rarely a winter goes by without the lifeboats having to battle against howling gales and treacherous waves to rescue crews in trouble.

The Revd James Williams and Frances, his wife, had arrived at their new parish of Llanfairynghornwy on just such a stormy day, when a sailing packet, the 'Alert' was driven on to the rocks close by and sank almost immediately with the loss of one hundred and forty lives. There was no boat to attempt a rescue.

The tragedy had such an effect upon James and Frances Williams that they vowed to set up an organisation to provide boats for rescue purposes, to be stationed around the island.

They lobbied those living on the island who had some influence – the gentry, the clergy, port officials and boat builders. Such was the Williams' own enthusiasm for the project that they themselves had provided a boat at Cemlyn, with James Williams as its first coxswain, a month before the Anglesey Association for the Preservation of Life from Shipwreck was formed in 1828.

The need was desperate. In 1833 over fifty vessels were lost on the shores of Anglesey. In the twenty-seven years between 1829 and 1856, when the Anglesey Association became part of the Royal National Lifeboat Institution, over four hundred lives were saved by Anglesey lifeboats.

Painting was one of Frances Williams' many talents. She had made a large oil painting of the occasion when George IV landed in Holyhead from Ireland, three years before, so she lithographed it and sold copies at seven shillings each in aid of the lifeboat project.

In addition to parish duties, James Williams helped to design lifeboats and rocket equipment.

His bravery was also recognised in 1835 when the Royal National Lifeboat Institution awarded him its Gold Medal for rescuing the crews of two ships off the north coast of the island. He repeated this act of bravery several times.

Frances Williams was equally intrepid. She sailed with her husband in the Cemlyn boat across to the Skerries, where the lighthouse keeper was ill, attending him until she was sure he would improve, before returning to the mainland.

James Williams was a son of the Treffos estate, a nephew of Thomas Williams of The Mona Mine Company fame. He was a Canon and Chancellor of Bangor Cathedral.

The rectory of Llanfairynghornwy became a cultural centre during their occupancy, where James and Frances Williams, painted, read, played the harp and studied geology. They were eager to introduce every improvement in farming methods to their agricultural parishes.

James Williams is buried in Llanfairynghornwy church yard.

# William Owen Stanley (1802-1884)

When parishioners of St Cybi's church, Holyhead, celebrated the centenary of the opening of the Stanley Chapel, they remembered William Owen Stanley, one of the town's most generous benefactors.

The effigy of William Owen Stanley, lying flanked by angels on his tomb in the chapel, shows him to have been a handsome, strong-featured man.

He was born in Cheshire in 1802, one of twin sons of Sir John Thomas Stanley, the first Lord Stanley of Alderley. He married Elin, daughter of Sir John Williams of Bodelwyddan. Although he had been educated abroad and had travelled widely, Penrhos at Holyhead was his home, where he and his wife worked incessantly for the improvement of the quality of life in this corner of Anglesey.

He was Lord Lieutenant of Anglesey for thirty-four years, a Member of Parliament, a scholar and antiquary. For many years he was regarded as leader of the Anglesey Liberals.

On his death in 1884, the press was unstinting in its praise of this kindly man, referring to him as 'The grand old political chieftain, and one of the kindest and most considerate of landlords'.

William Owen Stanley and his wife assisted local charities to the tune of £30,000 during their lifetime. They founded and endowed The Stanley Hospital and Stanley Sailors' Home and a number of almshouses, and subscribed £3,000 for the restoration of St Cybi's church. They supplied Holyhead with water, erected the market, and contributed to the cost of the new church of St Seiriol as the town developed.

Among many other interests, William Owen Stanley wrote of the antiquities of Holy island for Archeologia Cambrensis, and his last pamphlet dealt with the vestiges of Roman workings for copper in Anglesey. He was a water-colour painter, and an enthusiastic gardener and naturalist.

Newspaper reports of his funeral paint a vivid picture. A huge crowd followed the slow-moving cortege as the hearse, drawn by a team of grey horses, proceeded from Penrhos to St Cybi's church where a guard of one hundred marines from H.M.S. Defence, with arms reversed, guarded the path to the church door. Flags in the harbour were lowered to half mast and every house curtain was drawn to a respectful close.

The house at Penrhos, William Owen Stanley's old home, has now been demolished, but wherever one goes in Holyhead there is some reminder of this 'grand old man' and the benefactor he was to his town.

*Angels guard the effigy of William Owen Stanley at*
*St Cybi's church, Holyhead*

# Sir Hugh Owen (1804-1881)

Hugh Owen started school at eight years old, and left when he was 17. He had no higher education. Yet he was largely responsible for setting up a committee to look into the state of secondary and higher education in Wales.

Hugh Owen was born at Y Foel, a farm near Tal-y-Foel at Llangeinwen. He was sent to a private school in Caernarfon and, at the age of 17, apprenticed to a Caernarfon saddler. The saddler's business closed down shortly after, and Hugh returned home to work on the farm.

His father organised the movement of cattle to London, and when Hugh was 21 he became a drover. It was the custom for a drover to be trusted with letters and packages for delivery in the city, and on one occasion Hugh Owen carried a letter to W. Bulkeley Hughes, a Welsh barrister known to his father, asking that the young man be found suitable work in London, to which Bulkeley Hughes agreed. He found Hugh Owen a post in the attorney's office of R. Vaughan Williams in Hatton Gardens, where he stayed for ten years.

In 1836 he moved to Somerset House, where he had been appointed under the newly established Poor Law Board, and so Hugh Owen became a civil servant. He was elevated to the post of chief clerk in 1853, and remained until he retired in 1872.

After living in London for some time, Hugh Owen began to compare educational opportunities in the city with those in Wales. He dreamed of being able to provide children of nonconformist parents with the same opportunities that were given to children whose parents were churchgoers – church schools already existed. There were private schools like the one

*The imposing statue to educationist Sir Hugh Owen, in The Square, Caernarfon, where his name is perpetuated in the name of the town's comprehensive school.*

in Caernarfon he had attended, and charity and privately funded grammar schools, but no nationally organised educational system existed, no training for teachers, no universities in Wales.

There had been a move to establish British Schools, but these were slow in reaching Wales. There were only two in north Wales and none in Anglesey. Hugh Owen was determined to tweak public conscience, so he sent a circular letter to those who had any influence in Wales – the clergy, the gentry, landowners and those with large private estates.

He made a fervent plea for support in his efforts.

The letter read . . .

'August 26, 1843

Dear Fellow Countryman,

You are conscious of the need to give your children an education, and you value freedom of conscience. To provide education, schools are essential; to safeguard freedom of conscience, the schools must be free of all connection with any religious sect.'

The letter went on to plead for the establishment of British Schools as the means to attain the end.

Ideally, the British Schools had to be given a Welsh image. So he suggested setting up The Cambrian Educational Society for promoting the establishment of day schools in Wales 'on the Principles of the British & Foreign Schools Society'. But his plans foundered through lack of financial support.

Undeterred, Hugh Owen used his high position in public service to lobby for two 'inspectors' to be appointed to visit areas in north and south Wales where there was an urgent need of schools, to advise on how to proceed. The Revd John Phillips did his work well in Anglesey for, between 1844 and 1846, schools were opened at Rhosybol, Marianglas, Cemaes and Llanrhuddlad. In 1856 Hugh Owen and others organised a conference in Bangor to discuss education and the seeds were sown there for a teachers' training college, which opened as Y

Coleg Normal in 1862.

The university college at Aberystwyth was opened in 1872, another dream realised by Hugh Owen, who was to be its benefactor to the end of his life.

He made a personal gesture to Wales, which was to be fruitful until 1894, by founding the North Wales Scholarship Association from his own resources, for boys from elementary schools in Anglesey.

An example of one who benefitted was the boy from Llannerchymedd elementary school who won a scholarship of £20 a year to attend a grammar school, which rose to £30 a year when he went on to higher education at Aberystwyth.

As well as his work for education, Hugh Owen was interested in the development of the National Eisteddfod and the Cymmrodorion Society. His association with the London Welsh Society resulted in the founding of The London Welsh Charitable Aid Society.

Hugh Owen was knighted in 1881, but died three months later at Mentone. He was buried in London.

A statue of Sir Hugh Owen stands on Y Maes in the town where he received his education, Caernarfon, and the town's comprehensive school bears his name.

# Sir William Roberts (1830-1899)

One of ten children of Sarah and Dr David Roberts, the well-known physician of Bodedern, William was to follow his father in his choice of career, but was to succeed in a much wider sphere.

As was the case with middle class families in the early years of the 19th century, he received his primary education at home with a family tutor, proceeding to the National School at Bodedern and then, as a boarder, to Mill Hill School in London.

In 1849 he became a medical student at London University where he graduated B.A. in 1851, M.B., in 1853 and M.D., in 1854. He spent part of his university years in France and Germany.

Meanwhile one of his brothers had moved to Manchester where he had been successful in establishing a drapery business, to be joined by more of the family as the wholesale warehouse flourished to become one of the most important merchanting centres in that rapidly growing city.

Manchester also had an infirmary and a medical school of expanding repute. It was the ideal centre for a young doctor, freshly graduated and full of ambition. These two attractions made William Roberts decide to apply for the post of house physician at the Manchester Royal Informary where he was appointed in 1854.

During those early years in Manchester he met, fell in love with, and married Elizabeth Johnson.

These were golden days for the young doctor, and advancement was rapid. He became an honorary physician at the hospital in 1855, and also lecturer in anatomy and

74

physiology at the Royal School of Medicine in Manchester, later to form an important department of the university.

In 1861 he lectured to medical students on pathology and in 1863 on the principles and practice of medicine.

William Roberts maintained his association with the Infirmary until 1883.

By this time, he was regarded as one of the most able and knowledgeable in his profession, at home and abroad, through his keen and careful research and the application of his findings, his lectures, and his publications which were many and varied.

He wrote treatises on urinary and rectal diseases, digestive ferments, dietetics and dyspepsia. He was elected Fellow of the Royal College of Physicians in 1865 and a Fellow of the Royal Society in 1877.

The ultimate accolade in his profession came in 1897 when he was invited to give the Harveian Oration before the Royal College of Surgeons when he chose 'Science and Modern Civilization' as his subject.

William Roberts was knighted in 1885, for his services to medicine.

After twenty four years in Manchester, Sir William Roberts moved to London and the last twenty years of his long and busy life, although he was officially retired, were spent there and at his estate, Y Bryn, Llanymawddwy, where he sat on the Meirionnydd bench.

He was regarded as one of the shining lights of his age in medicine, a superb teacher and a man of great integrity.

Sir William Roberts died in London in 1899, and was buried in the churchyard at Llanymawddwy.

# Lewis William Lewis (Llew Llwyfo) (1831-1901)

One of the most gifted Welshmen of the 19th century was born at Penysarn, Llanwenllwyfo, on March 31, 1831, to Richard and Mary Lewis. Richard was a miner, Mary the daughter of a schoolmaster. Lewis William Lewis received little education and went to work alongside his father in the Mynydd Parys copper mine when he was only eight years old. Even then, he liked singing and would keep the miners entertained.

The family moved to Bangor when the railway was being built, and Richard Lewis found work on the tunnels at each end of Bangor station. Young Lewis was apprenticed to a grocer and draper who occupied Siop Goch on the corner of Dean Street.

This was the era when literary societies were springing up through a burgeoning of interest in poetry and writing poetry according to the strict Welsh metres. In 1847 a society had been formed in Llannerchymedd. Three years later Lewis, with two Anglesey friends, launched another in Amlwch.

When Lewis' family moved to Bangor, Lewis joined a Bangor society. He began to write for the press while in Bangor. In 1850 he went to work in John Lewis' draper's shop in London House, Holyhead, and met his future wife, 'Miss Hughes from St Asaph'.

They married in 1851 and the couple moved back to Penysarn where Lewis opened a draper's shop. But his mind was on literature, poetry and music, and he turned to journalism, the business taking second place.

The next few years found him in the hurry and bustle of the newspaper world, first at Holywell where he worked as sub editor on the church newspaper, Y Cymro. In 1855 he became

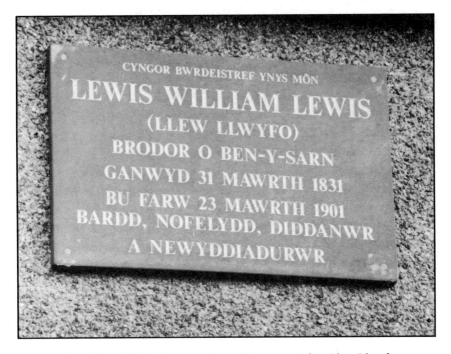

*The village hall at Penysarn bears this memorial to Llew Llwyfo*
*– 'poet, novelist, entertainer and journalist'.*

editor of Amserau, a Welsh paper which was published in Liverpool. Later he joined Y Faner in Denbigh, Y Gwladgarwr in Aberdare, and then he spent some time in Caernarfon working for Yr Herald Gymraeg and Y Genedl Gymraeg, all Welsh newspapers of note.

Lewis William Lewis probably contributed more to the Welsh newspaper press than anyone else in his time.

He did not confine himself to newspapers. He also wrote articles for Y Gwyddoniadur (encyclopedia) and the more important magazines published in Wales. He was a poet of some note (his bardic name was Llew Llwyfo) and he produced novels with a temperance theme – a strange quirk for a man who was not averse to carousing in the public houses of Caernarfon.

In 1868 Llew Llwyfo published a selection of his poems, Gemau Llwyfo (Llwyfo's Gems), and over the years he accumulated a long succession of Eisteddfod literary successes.

There was a large Welsh community on the east coast of America, and Lewis went over to become co-editor of their Welsh paper, Y Wasg (The Press) staying for four years the first time. He made a second visit later.

Lewis William Lewis was not only famous for the written word. He had a stage presence and a pleasant singing voice. Music was one of his many interests. Along with others he organised concerts in Wales and America, and conducted the proceedings at many eisteddfodau. His charisma made him a favourite throughout Wales and with the Welsh contingent in America.

But Lewis William Lewis had sad final years. He was struck by paralysis at 47 years of age, and spent his last years in comparative poverty, part of the time in Llangefni workhouse. He died at his son's home in Rhyl in March 1901, and is buried in Llanbeblig cemetery in Caernarfon, the town where he did so much of his work.

He is still remembered in Penysarn, by a plaque on the village hall.

# Samuel Jonathan Griffith (1850-1893)

Samuel Jonathan Griffith, whose bardic name was 'Morswyn', was born in Holyhead on June 6, 1850.

He had more than the usual educational opportunities, as for a time he studied medicine in Dublin, but as far as is known he went no further than one examination.

At home in Holyhead in his youth he attended Tabernacl Independent Chapel where he became leader of the congregational singing. When the Independent chapels split, he left Tabernacl and founded another in Holyhead where he was a deacon and conducted the singing there, too.

In 1881, with a partner, he launched the weekly Holyhead Mail which was edited in Caernarfon where he was assistant editor for a time.

A contemporary described him as a superb literary man, an intelligent musician. He supported eisteddfodau and cultural events in the chapels. He composed songs for children – said to have been done for them to sing at election times when he showed staunch Liberal tendencies.

It is as the composer of the hymn Craig yr Oesoedd that he is best known to today's Welsh chapelgoers. This hymn was said to have been inspired by the rocky coastline at Porth Dafarch, where a plaque to his memory has been erected. The hymn compares God with the Rock of Ages, a shelter in every storm.

Samuel Jonathan Griffith died at Holyead in 1893 and was buried at Maeshyfryd cemetery.

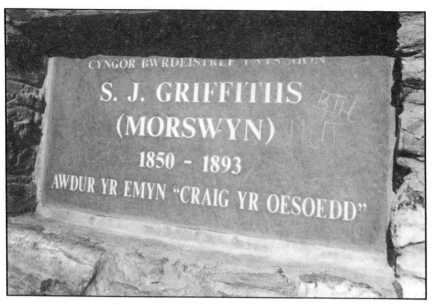

*The plaque to Samuel Jonathan Griffith at Porth Dafarch*

*The rocky coastline at Porth Dafarch which inspired the hymn*
*'Craig yr Oesoedd' (Rock of Ages)*

# Sir Ellis Jones Ellis-Griffiths (1860-1926)

A Liberal Member of Parliament for Anglesey who strongly supported the disestablishment of the church in Wales as he believed in the right of the individual in religious matters, Sir Ellis Jones Ellis-Griffiths held the seat for twenty-three years. Although chairing parliamentary committees and being under-secretary at the Home Office for a time, his parliamentary career fell short of brilliance, due, it was said, to his never having the ability to reach his potential because of a lack of self-confidence.

Ellis Jones Griffiths, as he then was, was born in Birmingham, the son of a successful Welsh builder, Thomas Morris Griffiths, who retired shortly after Ellis was born, and the family came to live at Tŷ Coch, Brynsiencyn. His early schooldays were spent at Brynsiencyn and at a private school in Holt, near Wrexham. From there he went as one of the first students to the newly opened university college at Aberystwyth, where he first became interested in politics.

Ellis was a keen scholar, and gained his London University Bachelor of Arts degree when he was only 19. From Aberystwyth he proceeded to Cambridge, through a Downing College scholarship, to study law.

He gained his first class Law Tripos in 1883 and was accepted to the Middle Temple the following year. By 1887 Ellis Jones Griffith was well on the way to a promising law career. He was called to the Bar in 1887. From 1888 until 1892 he was a Fellow of Downing College.

While a student at Cambridge he had been President of the Union in 1886, its first Welsh-speaking President, and was noted for easy fluency, a sparkling wit, and a succinct turn of phrase.

He was invited to stand as prospective parliamentary candidate for West Denbighshire, but refused because he did not feel he was wealthy enough to shoulder the financial burden.

The health of his wife, Mary, and their three children was precarious for some years.

But politics continued to attract, and he was a frequent speaker on political platforms. He had contested, unsuccessfully, against the Conservatives in Toxteth, but three years later, in 1893, he was elected Liberal candidate for Anglesey and won the election.

At the time of the Boer War, anti-war feeling was running high in Gwynedd, but Ellis Jones Griffiths stood out firmly in favour, at the risk of losing support. The next election saw him returned once more, and support for him was solid until 1918.

Ellis Jones Griffiths' parliamentary career was underlined by his firm belief in the disestablishment of the church in Wales, and he worked constantly towards steering the Act through the House of Commons. As was to be expected, this stance was unpopular with the clergy of his consistuency who held meetings to oppose disestablishment, accusing their Member of self-interest rather than a desire to promote the welfare of Wales. But their protests went unheeded.

When the Tories were in power, Ellis strongly criticised their education plans for Wales. Overseas problems caught his attention. He supported the Anglo-Russian Treaty of 1908, and the following year he was one of the few who stood out for the political rights of the coloured population of South Africa. he was also in favour of votes for women in this country.

Ellis Jones Griffiths was chairman of two parliamentary commitees, one on industrial and reform schools, and the other on industrial diseases.

The final parliamentary accolade came in 1914 when he was appointed a member of the Privy Council, and was created a baronet in 1918. When knighted, he changed his name to Sir Ellis Jones Ellis-Griffiths. That year he lost his Anglesey seat to the Labour candidate, Sir Owen Thomas.

Although invited to contest again in 1920, he refused. He was elected in 1923, however, as Member for Carmarthen but soon made way for his successor, Sir Alfred Mond.

In his early days as a barrister, and later after resigning from the Cabinet in 1915, he was busy on the circuits in London, Chester and north and south Wales. He served as Recorder for Birkenhead in 1907-12, becoming King's Counsel in 1910.

Sir Ellis Jones Ellis-Griffiths died while on circuit in Swansea in 1926. He is buried at Llanidan churchyard, Brynsiencyn.

# John Owen Jones (Ap Ffarmwr) (1861-1899)

Although a plaque to John Owen Jones is attached to the wall of the school at Dwyran where he received his early education, he was born at Ty'n Morfa, Trefdraeth, in 1861. His father died when John was four years old, and eventually his mother married again and the family went to live at Cae'r Llechan, a farm at Dwyran, where he stayed until he was fourteen.

His working life began when he became apprenticed to Lewis Lewis at the Nelson Emporium in Caernarfon, a large drapery store.

Life in Caernarfon was very different to life in a quiet Anglesey village. Welsh life in the town offered a great deal to an impressionable teenager, and young John Owen Jones found himself drawn in to many of the religious, social and cultural activities that were fashionable at the end of the 19th century. He joined Moriah chapel, one of the largest and most active nonconformist chapels. He was an avid reader, and began reading English journals and magazines to widen his horizons.

Lewis Lewis gave every support to his apprentices to enjoy a rich cultural life in what little spare time they had, and encouraged literary discussion as a popular means of entertainment. Literary societies were springing up in the chapels – John Owen was a founder member of the society launched in Moriah Chapel in 1877 – and there was even a literary society associated with The Nelson for the benefit of the staff.

Caernarfon was the place to be during this great surge of enthusiasm for the written word. Bookshops in the town were places where people met to discuss books and any topic, political or literary. Even an impecunious apprentice was welcomed if he had something to say or was willing to listen. It did not matter if he could not afford to buy.

But the time came when John Owen Jones received a legacy, which he decided to use to educate himself. He chose to spend a year at Dr John S. Kirk's private school in Caernarfon to prepare himself before proceeding to the University College at Aberystwyth in 1880, to study for three years.

His choice of Kirk's school may have been prompted by the advertisement which read . . .

'Pupils at this establishment are carefully grounded in all those branches which constitute a Liberal Education. They are trained to THINK on the subject they study and learning by mere rote is avoided as much as possible.'

Except for the study of English, it is not known what subjects John Owen Jones read at Aberystwyth, nor in the year following at Owen's College, Manchester. There was a close association between Aberystwyth and Owen's in those days which resulted in many Welsh students completing their education in Manchester.

While in Manchester, John Owen Jones entered into the Welsh life of the town and could well have been influenced, too, by the Liberalism of the day, as reflected in 'The Manchester Guardian'.

In 1884 the one-time drapery apprentice began the career which was to bring him fame – journalism. He was appointed the first full-time parliamentary reporter for a Welsh language newspaper, Y Genedl Gymreig, whose head office was in Caernarfon. For some time he was based in London where he met members of parliament and discussed problems with them which were reported in his column.

Life had taken him away from Anglesey for a while, but, on returning to Caernarfon to work later, he began to be keenly interested in the social problems besetting Anglesey farm labourers, and used the newspaper colums to bring those problems to the notice of his readers. For this, he used the pseudonym Ap Ffarmwr (Son of a Farmer).

John Owen Jones returned to live in his old home, Cae'r Llechan in Dwyran, and while continuing his full-time reporting locally, he also opened a higher grade school in the village, where Greek, Latin, French, English and Mathematics were taught. He did this until 1890 by which time it was known as Llangeinwen Grammar School, and shorthand and business studies were added to the curriculum.

After a while, his interest in teaching began to pall. The pull of journalism was stronger. He began to contribute to Y Cymro, eventually being offered the editorship, which he declined. Instead he chose an editorial post with the Welsh National Newspaper Company in Caernarfon in 1890. This allowed him a wider platform to pursue his efforts on behalf of the Anglesey farm labourers, in an attempt to encourage them to band together to improve their working conditions and give them shorter working hours. With the experience of different life-styles behind him, comparisons sharpened. Farm labourers in other parts of Britain were forming trade unions in an attempt to better their lot – why not those in Anglesey?

On the island the gap between master and servant was wider than elsewhere, due in some part, he maintained, to the large size of many Anglesey farms. Labourers were hearing of higher wages to be earned in the Caernarfon slate quarries, and were crossing the Menai Strait to find work there, returning home at weekends. They brought home news of the Quarryworkers Union' activities, and they began to compare their hours of work with the fourteen hour day they had left behind on the farm.

John Owen Jones worked long and hard and wrote thousands of words in an effort to spark opinion into activity, and to persuade farmers that their labourers' hours of work must be cut and their wages increased.

Through his column in one newspaper, Y Werin, a meeting was convened in Llangefni on Easter Monday, 1890, which did result in a shorter working day, but little more, and the impetus was not maintained to carry on the fight.

He left Caernarfon in 1894 to become editor of the Merthyr Times and later in the same year, to edit the Nottingham Express. John Owen Jones died in Nottingham in 1899. His body was brought back to Anglesey to be buried at Dwyran.

The monument raised to him bears the inscription ' . . . by the agricultural workers of Anglesey (mainly) to honour remembrance of him for upholding our rights so successfully through the press'.

# Sir John Morris-Jones (1864-1929)

A slate plaque in the garden wall of Tŷ Coch, Llanfairpwll, is a constant reminder to passers-by of an Anglesey boy who, from troubled beginnings, emerged to be one of Wales' finest Welsh language scholars.

John Morris-Jones' father had been a teacher at schools in Dwyran and Gaerwen, before setting up a small retail business in Llandrygarn where John was born in 1864. Three years later the family moved to Llanfair Pwllgwyngyll where there were better prospects at Siop Stesion, on the main Holyhead road. John first attended The Duchess of Kent School, a small church school. He went on to the Board school in the village, and later to Friars School in Bangor.

When the headmaster of Friars, Dr Lloyd, moved to oversee Christ's College, Brecon, some of the boys accompanied him, John among them. But he fell ill during 1879 and had to stay at home for the rest of the year. His father died the same winter, and John had to help his mother in the shop. Prospects of any further education looked bleak until Dr Lloyd wrote to his mother to ask that the boy should return to school under a generous scholarship.

John returned to Brecon where he was trained with Oxford entrance in view. He won a scholarship to Jesus College to read mathematics in 1883.

John Morris-Jones graduated in 1887, but by this time another discipline had completely taken over his life.

During the time he was at home following his father's death he had developed an interest in Welsh poetry, which he would read whenever he had the opportunity.

At Oxford he met other Welsh students with similar interests. In 1886 they banded together to form Cymdeithas Dafydd ap Gwilym where they could meet to converse in Welsh, and read and discuss Welsh poetry and literature. These were heady days for John Morris-Jones, and he found himself becoming disenchanted with the idea of earning his living through mathematics.

Sir John Rhys was Professor of Celtic Studies at Oxford. John was awarded the Meurig Scholarship which allowed him to stay at Oxford for another year to study under him.

In 1889 John returned to Wales to take a lectureship in Welsh at the University College in Bangor. Six years later he was elevated to the Chair and, from then, all his energies were channelled into making the department a centre of excellence.

He went back to Llanfair Pwllgwyngyll to live, building the imposing red brick house he was to occupy for the rest of his life. When asked what it would be called, it is said he replied that he would wait to her how the children of the village would name it as it was being built – and Tŷ Coch it was. John Morris-Jones married a local girl, Mary Hughes.

After the University was founded in 1894, Welsh classes had become popular. There is no doubt that John Morris-Jones influenced a changed attitude of contemporary Welshmen towards their language and literature. He began a new era in the history of Welsh literature through his teaching, through press writing, and from the Eisteddfod platform where he appeared on many occasions as adjudicator in literary competitions. He cleaned up the language, regenerating its purity. He worked towards bringing order to the strict metres in poetry and presenting them to a new school of poets.

John Morris-Jones' great contribution to the renaissance of Welsh in the early years of the century was his Welsh Grammar, Historical and Comparative, a volume of five hundred pages which brought order to chaos.

In 1921 came 'Elementary Welsh Grammar' and in 1925, Cerdd Dafod a book on the Welsh poetry systems.

In his busy academic life he edited cultural journals, had an interest in old manuscripts, calligraphy and fine printing, and learned Persian so that he could translate 'Omar Khayam' into Welsh.

Art and music captured his interest, too, in his more relaxed moments.

He enjoyed working with metal. The electric clock he made for his home, for which he cut every wheel himself, and designed the face and hands, worked perfectly.

John Morris-Jones was knighted in 1918. In 1919 he received an honours doctorate from Glasgow University, and in 1929 another from the National University of Ireland.

Sir John Morris-Jones died in Llanfair Pwllgwyngyll in 1929 and is buried in St Mary's churchyard.

He will be remembered for succeeding in his efforts to standardise the orthography of the Welsh language and restoring its syntax. His influence on the Welsh language of his time, and since, was and remains considerable.

*Tŷ Coch, the home in Llanfair Pwllgwyngyll of Sir John Morris Jones, to whom there is a plaque near the entrance gate.*

# Thomas Jesse Jones (1873-1950)

Thomas Jesse Jones was born in Llanfachraeth on August 4, 1875, the son of Benjamin Jones, saddler, and his wife Sarah, daughter of the local smith. When Sarah's father died, her mother became keeper of 'Y Bedol Aur', the inn in Llanfachraeth. When Benjamin Jones died at the age of 38, Sarah joined her mother and brought up her family at the inn. She had two sons and two daughters. Thanks to the generosity of customers, the children had a comfortable upbringing. T h e inn was the place where visiting ministers, educators and government officers made their headquarters, and the villagers and farmers met to while away an hour and to discuss their problems. 'Y Bedol Aur' was a forerunner of what we would regard today as a community centre.

Sarah had a good command of the English language, and was an intelligent woman with a vigorous personality. She was able to represent and defend the monoglot Welsh labourers in their legal wrangles with landlords and public officers, and was well respected.

In 1884 the lives of Sarah and her family took an abrupt turn when they decided to emigrate and sail for America, to make their home in Middleport, Ohio, close to Sarah's brother who was in business there. This proved to be a wise move, for in Ohio the boys received a good education, and by 1891 Thomas was reading for a degree at Washington and Lee (Virginia) Universities and by 1904 he had graduated M.A., B.D., and Ph. D. from Marietta and Columbia Universities and the Union Theological Seminary in New York.

Social conditions proved of great interest to young Thomas

*The chapel at Pont yr Arw, Llanfachraeth, to which Thomas Jesse Jones presented a bible in memory of his parents.*

Jesse Jones, in a country where immense social changes were taking place following the American Civil War.

He became a social researcher in New York, and was appointed chief officer of the University's Social Foundation. By 1904 he had accepted the post of vice chaplain and research organiser in the Hampton Normal and Agricultural Institute, Virginia, founded in 1868 by the American Missionary Society as part of an effort to integrate blacks and whites by offering educational opportunities to negroes to enable them to fulfil the new responsibilities which faced them on becoming free men in society.

The Institute had a high reputation, its aims being 'to make the pupil a willing and a good worker and able to teach his trade to others'. Boys and girls were accepted, and trained in agriculture, horticulture, librarianship, domestic science and craft.

Still a young man, these were formative years for Thomas Jesse Jones, years which made a great impression on him, and when the education of negroes became the main aim of his life. The framework for his future thought and activity was based on this.

He had high ideals – the care of health and cleanliness, respect for the environment, the standard of family life, and the importance of leisure as a means of introducing richness to that family life.

Throughout his working days, Thomas Jesse Jones published widely on the subjects closest to his heart, beginning with The Sociology of a New York Block in 1904, when he looked into the social implications of close contact in city life.

He remained at the Hampton Institute until 1909, when he left to join the Federal Government in Washington as chief statistician, dealing mainly with statistics relating to blacks and whites in the U.S. population, and he soon came to be regarded as an expert in this field.

Then came yet another change when, in 1913, he was appointed education director to the Phelps-Stokes Foundation,

*Pont yr Arw chapel, Llanfachraeth*

CYNGOR BWRDEISTREF YNYS MÔN
THOMAS JESSE JONES
1873 – 1950
Y BEDOL, LLANFACHRAETH
ADDYSGWR A DYNGARWR
"Gwyn eu byd y rhai addfwyn
Canys hwy a etifeddant y ddaear"

*The plaque on the chapel wall refers to Thomas Jesse Jones as*
*'Educator and Philanthropist'.*

a post he held until his retirement in 1946.

The Phelps-Stokes Foundation, like Thomas Jesse himself, had high ideals. It was set up 'in the firm belief that the peace and welfare of the world can never be assured until conditions in every country, no matter how small or how remote from world centres of population, are reasonably satisfactory'.

He must have experienced echoes of his first publication when he became involved in the main purpose of the Foundation at the time he joined – 'the erection of tenement dwellings in New York City for the poor families of New York City and for educational purposes in the educating of negroes, North American Indians and needy white students'.

His main report under the auspices of the Fund came in 1917, in two volumes, dealing with negro education in the United States, and a study of private and higher schools for coloured people in the United States.

The year 1917 saw America drawn into the First World War, and Thomas Jesse Jones was invited to go to France as a welfare officer with special responsibility for negro soldiers. His time in the war zone brought him into contact with Christian leaders in Europe and especially those sympathetic to the cause of the black man, a period of intense interest to him which widened his horizons still further.

On return to America when the war ended, he became one of the leaders of the American Baptist Mission with particular interest in education in the mission field. A conference of American missionary societies decided to study the state of education in Africa, and Thomas Jesse Jones was invited to head a delegation and chair a research commission. The commission spent a year in central, south and west Africa and, in 1922, published a report which had a tremendous impact, to which the various governments involved gave their blessing.

The stipulation that language should be respected led to the languages of the many tribes being declared the official language of the local school, followed by the gradual introduction of the language of the prevailing government

(English, French, Portuguese, etc.).

Resulting from the 1922 report, another commission was sent, this time to East Africa in 1924, when French Somaliland, Abyssinia, Kenya, Uganda, Tanganyika, Zanzibar, Portuguese East Africa, Nyasaland, Northern and Southern Rhodesia and South Africa were visited. The commission's report on this visit appeared in 1925.

By this time there was nobody more influential on educational matters in the colonies than Thomas Jesse Jones. His work was recognised by the League of Nations, and the governments of Britain, France and the United States.

During his busy life, he published The Alley Houses of Washington, Tuberculosis among the Negroes, Negroes and the Census and The Navajo Indian Problem, all of them works which reflected his clear outlook on the social problems of the time.

The British government set up the Colonial Education department following his African reports, and honoured him with a dinner in Lancaster House in 1925.

During 1932 he lectured in African Universities under the Carnegie Foundation, and in 1937 headed yet another commission, this time to study Navajo Indians in America.

After his death in January 1950, friends and colleagues the world over paid tribute to his character and his work. Testimonials showed him to have been a man of outstanding talent, small in frame but energetic, with a sense of humour. He was, they said, someone quick to recognise a difficult situation, and ready to deal with it.

Although he had left behind his early life at Llanfachraeth, he never forgot his roots, and presented a bible in remembrance of his mother and father to the chapel at Pont yr Arw, where they had worshipped, in 1933.

# W.D. Owen (1874-1925)

Folklore and local tradition have often sparked an idea for a novel, and no Welsh writer followed this course more successfully than W.D. Owen, the Anglesey solicitor-writer whose only novel, Madam Wen, has remained popular for seventy five years.

He was born at Tŷ Franen, Bryngwran, the son of William and Jane Owen, in 1874. William died when his son was a small child.

After attending the Board school in Bryngwran, young William became a pupil teacher there, and later at Garth, Bangor. He then went for teacher-training to Y Coleg Normal in Bangor where he was awarded a first class certificate within two years.

W.D. Owen's first teaching post was at Clay Cross in Derbyshire, where he met his wife, Gwendoline Empsell who edited a woman's magazine and was an author.

But he found teaching unfulfilling and left Clay Cross school to spend some time as a journalist, no doubt encouraged by his wife. He turned from that career, too, to study law.

On being called to the Bar, he began to suffer ill health and was advised to return to the cleaner air of his native Anglesey. He and his wife settled at Rhosneigr, not far from his old home, in the hope that this health and that of his wife who was also a semi-invalid by this time, would improve.

For a time, W.D. Owen managed the Army Pensions Office in Llangefni, then opened his own solicitor's practice with offices in Llangefni and Rhosneigr.

These were the years when Anglesey was beginning to be

*Peaceful Llyn Traffwll, the setting for W.D. Owen's novel, 'Madam Wen'.*

tourism-conscious and villages like Rhosneigr, situated on the beautiful west coast with stunning seascapes and sandy beaches, were starting to sell themselves through colourful brochures.

W.D. Owen had a journalistic hand in the official guide to Rhosneigr, where he not only extolled the glories of the coastal scenery but also reminded would-be visitors of the fascinating lake district lying behind, an area full of mystery and folklore. He wrote of the character known by every child brought up in the district, Madam Wen, and described her as 'the famous Lady Robin Hood of North Wales'.

As soon as he had settled again in Anglesey, W.D. Owen had begun to write a novel, Dychweliad y Crwydryn (The Return of the Wanderer) which was serialised in weekly parts in the newspaper, Y Genedl Gymreig. It was a story describing life in an Anglesey village. When this had finished, the first part of Madam Wen, Arwres yr Ogof (Madam Wen, Heroine of the Cave) began, and this appeared weekly until July 1914.

Eleven years later, this was published as a book. A second edition appeared in 1965, and a third, edited with the language brought up to date by Professor Bedwyr Lewis Jones, in 1983.

The novel tells the story of Einir Wyn, a beautiful woman who had lost her inheritance as a result of the Civil War and, as Madam Wen, led a group of thieves before falling in love with Morys Williams, the squire of Cymunod, a local farm. The story has all the elements of romantic fiction, fast moving action, murderers, smugglers, the law, loves and hates and jealousies, all based on the lakeland area behind the wild, west coast of Anglesey which the author knew so well.

Madam Wen's cave is reputed to be on the shore of Llyn Traffwll, close to Llanfihangel-yn-Nhowyn.

# W.E. Williams (1881-1962)

Early experiments in flying are recorded on a plaque on the picnic site on Llanddona Beach, close to where a Caernarfonshire man built and flew an aeroplane in 1913.

William Ellis Williams was a quarryman's son from Bethesda, Dyffryn Ogwen, born in 1881. Attending the local school, he was found to have outstanding ability in mathematics and went on to the University in Bangor to read physics.

The area of particular interest to him was the stability of aeroplane gliders, and during his research he built small gliders which he fitted with pieces of magnesium. He would light these immediately before launching them, so that the flight path could be recorded on camera. This allowed the velocity to be calculated.

Following his student days in Bangor, and his degree, Ellis Williams researched in Glasgow and in Munich, where he collaborated with Dr Röntgen who discovered X-rays.

In 1906 Ellis Williams returned to Bangor as assistant lecturer in physics at the University. More experimenting took place and, in order to continue aerodynamic reasearch, he planned to build his own aeroplane, a monoplane made of light-weight woods – ash and bamboo – to weigh about 70 lbs.

In those days, as now, money for research was hard to find but Ellis Williams' obsession caught the interest of local wealthy ship-builder, Henry Rees Davies of Treborth, whose contribution of £50 (quite a considerable sum in those days) was the first towards hiring an engine for the aircraft.

Then came the problem of where to build and where to try to fly the aeroplane. Again, a local man came to the rescue. Sir

Harry Verney owned land at Llanddona, and he allowed Ellis to use a field where he could build a temporary hangar, close to a stretch of very firm sand where the machine could be tested.

Building took some time, and Williams more or less lived on site during the building, testing and re-testing until he felt all was ready for the flight. An engine had been hired from A.V. Roe.

The plaque records that the test flight in September 1913 was successful, when Ellis Williams achieved a height of seven feet, the 'Bamboo Bird', as it was called, flying at 37 miles per hour.

Further research came to a halt when war was declared in 1914. Williams gave unique war service at the Vickers factory at Brooklands, where his expertise was invaluable.

After the Armistice he returned to Bangor. By this time new challenges were on the horizon, and he turned his attention to hydro electricity and radio.

Thirty years after being appointed assistant lecturer at Bangor, William Ellis Williams became the first Professor of Electrical Engineering in the University of Wales. He retained his Chair in Bangor until his retirement, which he spent where he began, in Dyffryn Ogwen. He died there in 1962, aged 81.

*The memorial to William Ellis Williams, 'mathematician and engineer',
reminds visitors to Llanddona beach of his aero-nautical experiments.*

# Sir Ifor Williams (1881-1965)

Although Ifor Williams was not born in Anglesey, he lived in Menai Bridge long enough for him to be regarded as an Anglesey man.

He was born at Pendinas, Tregarth, the son of a quarryman and had his elementary education at Gelli and Llandegai schools before proceeding to Friars School, Bangor, in 1894.

After a year at Friars he had a serious accident which confined him to bed for six years with a back injury, from which he never recovered fully. But he did make sufficient progress to attend Clynnog College in 1901, where he studied for university entrance. He entered Bangor University to read classics and graduated with honours in Greek in 1905 and first class honours in Welsh the following year.

The head of the Welsh department at Bangor was John Morris-Jones, and Ifor Williams remained at the college as his assistant while he read for his Master's degree, which he received a year later. Three years later Ifor Williams received a personal Chair giving him the title Professor of Welsh Literature.

When Sir John Morris-Jones died in 1929, the Welsh Literature Chair and that for Welsh Language which had been held by Ifor Williams were combined, and Ifor Williams was given the new appointment.

He occupied this Chair until he retired in 1947, and he was then knighted for his services to the Welsh language.

Ifor Williams' life was busy. As well as lecturing, writing, giving radio talks, and performing all the tasks expected of a professor of an important university department, he was chairman of the Board of Celtic Studies of the University of Wales in 1941, and edited the language and literature section of the Board's Bulletin.

He was awarded the Cymmrodorion Medal in 1938, made a Fellow of the British Academy in the same year and a Fellow of the Society of Antiquaries of London in 1939.

The Royal Commission on Ancient Monuments in Wales and Monmouthshire appointed him a member in 1943, as did the Ancient Monuments Boards for Wales. And he acted as Curator of the Bangor Museum.

Ifor Williams helped to found the University of Wales Press in 1922.

He was held in great affection by people in every walk of life, as he was adept at speaking in public to an audience on any level. He wrote for the ordinary reader as well as the scholar, and his contribution towards understanding early Welsh literature and poetry and language is inestimable.

The late Tecwyn Lloyd, one of his students at Bangor, writing after his death in the literary journal Barn said there was never a university professor more personal in his attitude and more interesting in conversation than Sir Ifor. He talked, conversed, never lectured. His seminars were like fireside chats.

Spoken Welsh was one of his chief interests, along with the study of Welsh place-names. His book Enwau Lleoedd (Place-names) published in 1945, was a best-seller and remains popular to this day.

Through the results of his studious research, Sir Ifor Williams became a well-known and highly respected figure to students of Celtic languages throughout the world. But he also appealed, through his talks outside the university and over the air waves, to everyone interested in the language.

He preached in the local chapels in Anglesey and around Bangor every Sunday for many years, where his presentation was homely and clear. Humour and wit were never far away, even in the pulpit.

In 1913, Ifor Williams married Myfanwy Jones of Cae Glas,

Pontllyfni, and it was to Pontllyfni that he retired in 1947, and where he died.

During his working life he lived at 'Y Wenallt' in Porthaethwy, where there is a plaque to his memory.

# W. Bradwen Jones (1892-1970)

Bradwen Jones, one of Wales' most talented musicians of the 20th century, was born in Caernarfon in April 1892. His mother Elizabeth was a singer and a pianist. She and Bradwen's father were members of the prestigious choir, Côr Caernarfon, and it was to that choir's conductor, John Williams, that Bradwen went for his early music lessons.

He became a choirboy at the age of seven, at Christ Church, where John Williams was organist. For the next eight years Bradwen learned the discipline of church music, and had piano and organ lessons from his choirmaster.

He left school at the age of 14, and began work in a solicitor's office in the town. Then he was invited to work for the Glynllifon estate at Llandwrog, the great mansion home of the Hon. F.G. Wynn, and accepted eagerly, no doubt being attracted by the musical opportunities as the house possessed an organ and the family enjoyed music. It was part of the elegant way of life at Glynllifon.

Bradwen was given leave to take organ lessons from Dr Roland Rogers at Bangor Cathedral, making the eighteen miles journey by bicycle, whatever the weather. His tutor expected young Bradwen Jones to practise diligently, and he was not disappointed.

Another branch of the Wynn family lived at Rug, near Corwen. The house had a private chapel which was used regularly for services. Bradwen Jones was appointed organist to the family at the age of 18, and there he stayed for five years.

It was an enjoyable period in his life, when he could develop his musical talents. There was no evening service at Rug Chapel so he could play for evensong or Gosper at the church in Gwyddelwern nearby. He began to give recitals in and around Corwen, and formed a male voice choir whose concerts were very popular and received enthusiastic and encouraging press notices.

After eight years he was ready for a change, and applied for and was appointed to the post of organist and choirmaster at St Seiriol's church, Holyhead, taking up his duties in 1915.

A year later, he joined the Royal Welsh Fusiliers Reserve and was drafted to Park Hall Camp, Oswestry. There was opportunity for him to continue with his music-making in the Oswestry area, where he played the organ in local churches and gave recitals. In 1917 his company sailed for the Middle East, first to Palestine then to Egypt where he was commissioned the following year. He remained in Egypt after the war ended, conducting the 53rd division Welsh Male Voice choir, composing, and playing his own compositions in concerts and recitals in Alexandria.

After demobilisation Bradwen Jones returned to Holyhead where he experienced a period of poor health, but he found time to consolidate his professional qualifications by studying for diplomas from the Royal Academy of Music, the Royal College of Organists and Trinity College of London.

At this time he was also invited to be resident conductor of Côr Caernarfon, an honour which pleased particularly because of his family connections with the choir in the past. He also founded a Musical Society in Holyhead.

Bradwen Jones married in 1926. The 1930s were busy years for him, teaching, giving recitals and concerts, adjudicating and composing. He was music master at Trearddur House School for several years. He also produced Gilbert and Sullivan operas at Holyhead.

In 1952 he resigned from St Seiriol's, but was organist at Hyfrydle chapel until his death at the Stanley Hospital in 1970.

Bradwen Jones was a shy man who was difficult to know. He liked his own company, he had very high musical standards which he sought to impose on all his pupils.

He made a musical career for himself at a time when to do so successfully was difficult, as music was not generally taught in schools in his early days. He was a strict disciplinarian in all he undertook. But those who came under his influence spoke of 'a magic touch that had a profound effect upon his audience' and 'the way we sang the psalms was an inspiration to the congregation'.

His plaque can be seen in the Market Square at Holyhead.

*The bi-lingual plaque to musician William Bradwen Jones in the Market Square, Holyhead.*

# Ifor Owain Thomas (1892-1956)

Musician, photographer, artist – Ifor Owain Thomas was all three, but is remembered chiefly as a tenor.

He was the third child of Owen and Isabella Thomas, born at Bay View, Red Wharf Bay on April 10, 1892. Before her marriage his mother was a well known singer from Dyffryn Nantlle in Caernarfonshire. Following the birth of Ifor, the family moved to the Pandy at Pentraeth where his father wove cloth to sell at Llangefni market.

Young Ifor was educated at the local school and, when he left, apprenticed to a joiner. He sang as a child, receiving lessons from his mother and a Bangor teacher, E.D. Lloyd. He suffered from chronic asthma, which was to dog him all his life and be responsible for a change of career later.

His mother prompted him to compete in eisteddfodau, and when he did so at the Abergavenny National Eisteddfod in 1913 the adjudicator, Walford Davies, gave him every encouragement to continue with his music studies seriously, suggesting that he should apply for a place at one of the London music colleges.

Ifor Thomas won a scholarship to the Royal College of Music in 1914, the best from four hundred competitors. During the next four years, throughout the war period, he twice attempted to enter the army but was refused each time because of his health problem. After his college period in London he went to study in Paris and Milan, and sang in Milan, Monte Carlo and Nice.

In 1920 Ifor married and went to live at Worcester Park in Surrey where he and his wife, Ceridwen, had two children. One daughter died when she was small. In 1925 he made his only

Promenade appearance in the Royal Albert Hall, and recorded four opera excerpts. His opera debut had taken place in Milan the year previously when he sang the part of Dmitri in Boris Godunov, appearing with Chaliapin in the title role. He also sang with Caruso and Gigli.

Ifor Thomas did not see much of his home at Worcester Park in 1927/8, as he appeared at the Comedie Francaise and Paris Opera, then went to the United States for a five-month contract to join the Metropolitan Quartet of New York. He was smitten with America and the warmth of the reception he received there, so remained for a further year working in Pittsburgh.

In 1929 he returned on a visit to Anglesey. By this time his marriage had broken down and divorce was under way, so he chose to return to the United States where he had won the admiration of the Welsh community on the east coast.

It was not long before Ifor Thomas married for the second time. Mildred Unfried was a pianist, making radio commercials.

His asthma was becoming more of a hindrance to his career as a soloist. He continued to sing, when he could, with a male quartet called 'The Bohemians' and then formed his own group of Welshmen called 'The Four Aces' whose accompanist came from Holyhead. They were successful and in demand, and this, as well as conducting small choirs, kept him busy musically.

But all was not well, and at the end of 1933 Ifor Thomas' professional singing ended. For some time he had been interested in photography, and decided that this was to be his new career.

He obtained work with Collier's Magazine and during the next fifteen years, until his retirement, photographed many famous people including film stars and politicians, Roosevelt and Churchill among them.

During the 1940s he founded the Cymric Society of New York and was a member of the St David's Day Society.

In 1948, on his retirement from Collier's Magazine, he took up painting and was equally successful in this, exhibiting water colours and oil paintings in Britain and the United States.

In 1955, when he made his last visit to Anglesey, he spent some time in the Caernarfon & Anglesey Infirmary in Bangor, undergoing treatment for his asthma, but to little avail. Soon after his return home to America he died in New York on his birthday in 1956.

Those who remember Ifor Thomas remember his enthusiasm for Wales and for Anglesey in particular. He had the true emigrant's hiraeth (longing) for Wales. He changed his middle name from Owen to the Welsh form, Owain. Many Welsh people were welcomed to his home in New York, where he lived in exile but never forgot his roots. He was a member of the Presbyterian church there and conducted the Welsh Women's Choir in the city from 1944 until he died.

# Richard Huws (1902-1980)

Visitors to Liverpool during the 1960s would stop on the Goree Piazza to stare in amazement at the great water sculpture where huge metal buckets mounted on stanchions emptied water noisily into the pool below, to a pattern of movement which was mesmerising.

Those who had also visited the Festival of Britain in 1951 would recall a water sculpture there, on the South Bank, which drew similar attention.

But how many knew that both were the inspiration and creation of Richard Huws of Talwrn, engineer, sculptor, cartoonist and designer?

Richard Hughes (he was to revert to the Welsh form of his surname later) was born in Penysarn near Amlwch in 1902, the fifth of seven children of Thomas and Catherine Hughes. His father was then headmaster of Penysarn school, and later at Llangoed. Richard attended Beaumaris school, and while in his teens worked voluntarily with a local joiner.

A local businessman ordered two hundred hutches for his rabbits, and Richard amazed him by completing the order in two or three days. On enquiry, the customer found that Richard had invented a method of manufacture which was quick and economical, and surprisingly sophisticated for a teenager. This impressed him to such an extent that he promised to make every effort to procure an apprenticeship at the Merseyside shipbuilders, Cammel-Laird, if Richard would be interested.

This was forthcoming, and the new apprentice made such a success of his work at the Birkenhead shipyard that he was awarded a Cammel-Laird scholarship to study naval architecture at Liverpool University.

While he was at college, he was a regular contributor to the University magazine, for which he developed his early talent in drawing caricatures.

While still a student in the engineering department he attended art classes in his spare time, with the result that art began to take pride of place in his life.

He obtained a second class honours degree and was offered various posts in engineering. Although his scholarship bound him to Cammel-Laird at the time it was awarded, when he graduated in 1925 lack of orders was leading to lay-offs in the yard, and he had no trouble in disassociating himself. But engineering held little interest any longer.

At that time Plaid Cymru was formed, and Richard was a founder member. He changed his surname to Huws as evidence of his new association, and designed the Triban logo which was to be so well known in future years. But like many artists, he had a fundamental mistrust of organisations, and his adherence to the party ceased when he felt that Plaid Cymru was becoming too exclusive.

Wanting freedom and fresh experience, he decided to roam Europe, financing himself by his drawings and caricatures as he travelled, and he was successful.

He was persuaded to seek a place at the prestigious Kunstgewerbeschule in Vienna, and walked across France to Austria, supporting himself financially by selling his drawings, and raised enough to allow him to stay in Vienna to study sculpture for four years between 1927 and 1930.

He returned to London in 1930 where, a year later, he married Edrica Tyrwhitt, a fellow artist.

Throughout the 1930s Richard Huws worked and, despite the recession, he contributed to exhibition design, shop window dressing features, and, of course, his cartoons which could be seen in many newspapers and magazines.

The year 1938 saw him designing and constructing the massive Mechanical Man, a large working model of the human body, for the Glasgow Exhibition. This created much discussion and, no doubt, was one of the reasons why he was approached to contribute to the Festival of Britain in 1951.

The war years were to intervene. Richard Huws found himself once more behind the drawing board, as an inventor of aircraft components for Saunders Roe at Beaumaris, which allowed him to return to live in Anglesey. Among his inventions was a system which allowed aircraft to land safely in darkness. When hostilities ended in 1945 he returned to London and gave his time to producing a vertical water feature for the 'Sea and Ships' pavilion on the South Bank.

As happens to many artists, Richard Huws had his quiet times when work was slow in coming his way. One of those periods arose during the '50s when, to support his growing family, he had to find more mundane work. He returned to Saunders Roe but this time at Cowes, and without the stimulus of war which demanded special inspiration of an inventor-designer-engineer.

In 1955 he was appointed lecturer in design in the Department of Architecture at Liverpool University, so the family came back to Wales to live, this time to Llanrwst in Dyffryn Conwy where the children could absorb a Welsh way of life which Richard valued so much.

Richard Huws was not a qualified architect. His task was to design a first year course where he could combine all his engineering, industrial, art and landscape architecture experience, plus his own personal enthusiasm, and use his ability to give students a fresh slant to a subject.

He had always been interested in garden design and, while working on his various projects, he had found time to convert and improve gardens in the various homes he occupied, those of his friends and family, and anyone who would trust their land to his expertise. In the late 1940s he qualified for the Associateship of the Institute of Landscape Architects. He made every effort to awaken a sense of visual awareness in his students at Liverpool. A contemporary was of the opinion that his talents were not used to their full potential in the department.

Richard Huws believed that a creative visual sense could be learnt by anyone. He said

'It is commonly thought that such a sense ('The intuitive sense of pattern') depends upon having a rare and extraordinary gift, but in fact it depends much more on training. Some talent is essential, of course, but a great many of us have potential talent without being aware of it, simply because our sense of visual values has never been awakened.'

Between 1955 and 1970 Richard Huws took on a new career as industrial design consultant, and was one of the early members of a newly-founded post-war group, The Society of Industrial Artists.

When he retired he returned to Anglesey to live where his interests took on yet another new slant when he studied Welsh literature and philosophic and religious thought. He also renewed his plans for landscape and water features. He was physically active to the last. On the day he died he had been working in his garden at Bryn Chwilog, Talwrn. He is buried in Llanddyfnan.

The plaque to the memory of this talented engineer and artist is at Bryn Chwilog.

# Hugh Griffith (1912-1980)

Described at one of the finest King Lears in Shakesperian theatre, actor Hugh Griffith came late to the stage.

He was born in Marianglas in 1912, went to school locally then to Llangefni Grammar School before sitting examinations for a place at university. But he failed the English paper, so could not be admitted.

His father, William Griffith, persuaded him into the safe career of banking, and Hugh worked for a time at branches of the National Provincial in Llandudno, Llangefni, Mold and Abersoch.

While at Abersoch, he began to train young people in a drama group attached to the youth movement, Aelwyd yr Urdd. He still yearned for the stage. To get more experience he applied for a transfer to a London branch of the bank, which gave him the opportunity to attend night classes and to see plays, and also to perform with The People's Theatre in St Pancras, where a new play was performed each week.

He applied for a place at the Royal Academy of Dramatic Art, and came top out of three hundred applicants for a scholarship.

When he ended his studies there, he was awarded the Bancroft Gold Medal as the best Shakesperian actor of the year.

In 1939, when he left college, he went straight on to the West End stage, playing the part of Jimmy Farrell in The Playboy of the Western World at the Mercury Theatre. To follow, he played the Revd Dan Price in Jack Jones' Rhondda Roundabout.

During the second World War, Hugh Griffith served in India and Burma, and with a bomb clearance squad in south Wales. He was ill at Roehampton for some time after the war ended, but as soon as he recovered he joined the Shakespeare Memorial Theatre company in 1946, where he had a huge success playing King Lear.

In 1947, after the first London performance of The White Devil, his Cardinal Monticelso was given high praise by all the theatre critics. Although not the lead, he stole the show.

He then began to make films. And television followed, with Hugh Griffith playing the Revd John Williams in The Comedy of Good and Evil and the scientist in Quatermass.

Broadway attracted him, and he won an Oscar for his part as the Sheikh in Ben Hur in 1958.

The Criterion Theatre featured Waltz of the Toreadors which had a long run of two hundred and fifty performances before Hugh Griffith, as the lead, had a disagreement with the managers of the theatre, and refused to continue. Not for nothing did English actors in the West End look upon him as an 'enfant terrible' of the stage!

Hugh Griffith remained true to his Welshness throughout his career. He was outspoken, and had fixed ideas on how to play his characters. He was invited to adjudicate at the National Eisteddfod of Wales on one occasion, but was so uncompromising that he was not invited again.

His story had an ironic twist when, in the 1970s, the University College of Bangor honoured him with a D. Litt. degree, in spite of his inability to make the grade as a would-be student.

He died in 1980, and is remembered in Anglesey by a commemorative plaque at Marianglas school.

UN O'R ARDAL HON OEDD

HUGH GRIFFITH
1912 - 1980

A DDAETH YN ACTOR BYD-ENWOG
YMFALCHIAI BOB AMSER YN EI WREIDDIAU
TO COMMEMORATE AN OSCAR-WINNING ACTOR

*The memorial to Hugh Griffith at Marianglas School reminds the children
and passers-by that he 'became a world-renowned actor'
who was always proud of his roots.*

# John Roberts (1910-1984)

A deeply spiritual hymn-writer is certain to be appreciated by chapel-going Welshmen, particularly if he is equally expressive in the pulpit.

John Roberts, Llanfwrog, had both these qualities.

In fact, he wrote many more sermons than hymns and poems and was in demand throughout Anglesey and Gwynedd by congregations who appreciated his ability to convey a message simply, with complete sincerity. But his hymns, too, will remain pearls of the hymnbooks of many denominations when his sermons might have passed into oblivion.

He was born in Anglesey, at Llanfwrog, in 1910, close to the sea which held a fascination for him throughout his life. His early ambition was to go to sea but, instead, the year 1928 found him starting to preach. He attended school in Clynnog to prepare for university entrance, and recalled how he was introduced there to the poet, John Keats, whose work remained an inspiration to him all his life.

John Roberts spent six years at the University in Bangor, from 1931-7, graduating in the arts and divinity, and a final year as a post graduate in the Calvinistic Methodist college at Bala to hone his pastoral skills. He went on to serve churches in Carneddi (Bethesda), Y Garth (Porthmadog), Bala and Caernarfon before retiring in 1975 and returning to his old home in Llanfwrog.

His early introduction to Keats was followed by serious study of Shakespeare – he committed a great deal of Shakespeare's plays to memory. In his obituary to John Roberts, Dr Derec Llwyd Morgan says 'To him, the bard was a seer, a

*John Roberts, 'preacher and hymn writer', is remembered by the plaque at his village school.*

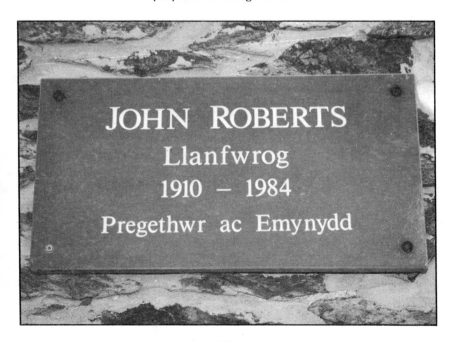

JOHN ROBERTS
Llanfwrog
1910 — 1984
Pregethwr ac Emynydd

visionary with a mastery of language and the ability to use language melodiously in order to convey to others the sense of life and through that to enrich mankind'. That ability he, too, conveyed so well in his own work.

John Roberts probably began to write poetry while in college. The Eisteddfod was the ideal place to gain helpful criticism, and success came early when he won the chair at Eisteddfod Dyffryn Ogwen in 1947, and again in 1956. When the National Eisteddfod of Wales came to Anglesey in 1983, he was chairman of its Literary committee.

From poetry it was only a small step to hymn writing, an obvious development for a minister of religion with a penchant for words and a fresh approach to moral, religious and social problems. It was his way of expressing his attitude to life's vicissitudes.

A collection of John Roberts' hymns, including verses for all occasions was published posthumously in 1987 under the title 'Glas y Nef'. He takes his rightful place among Anglesey worthies. He died in 1984 and is remembered by a plaque at the school, Ysgol Ffrwd Win.

# Charles Williams (1915-1990)

As defence against German submarine penetration of the Irish Sea during the First World War, the Admiralty proposed to fly airships from bases providing easy access, and one of these was planned on farmland three miles from Llangefni, between Bodffordd and the Holyhead Road. Its building entailed the demolition of small cottages, one of them being Penffordd, the birthplace of Charles Williams who was later to be a household name in the world of Welsh entertainment.

The family moved to Bodffordd, and a plaque to the memory of Charles Williams can be seen on Bodffordd school.

Family, friends and actor colleagues contributed their memories of him in a memorial book, published after his death. Those who knew Charles in his childhood describe him as a small boy, shy in informal company yet confident when he appeared on stage to recite in eisteddfod competitions. He was interested in verse speaking from an early age, and had a prodigious memory.

He was born into a family with a country background so it was natural that, on leaving school, he was employed at several farms as a labourer. He had a tough, wiry constitution, and could turn his hand to any kind of farm work. His first experience of living away from home, in a stable loft with other farm hands, came at around 15 years of age when he was taken on as a farmhand at Llanllechid, near Bangor. His mother went along with him on his first day, both riding bicycles. Young Charles was desperately homesick for a while, and looked forward to the days when he was instructed to herd animals to the market in Menai Bridge, so that he could meet up with some of his old Anglesey friends on the same errand from Anglesey farms.

The next few years saw him moving closer to home, to work on farms in the Gwalchmai area.

He was at ease mixing with the farming community, with whom he had great rapport, and it soon became obvious that he had an impish sense of humour, a lightning quick wit, and was never short of a word. He was always welcome at a chapel concert or on the eisteddfod platform. He knew instinctively how to approach an audience to whom he would appeal with his colloquial, unsophisticated humour.

Word of his abilities reached the ears of Sam Jones, head of BBC radio at Bangor, who invited him for audition and pronounced him 'a natural'. This resulted in a contract which allowed him to leave farm labouring as a permanent method of earning his bread and butter, and give his time to radio. But farming was in his bones, and he would go back to lend a hand whenever there was a need.

This new turn in his life also allowed him more time to train three speech choirs, produce one-act plays for a local drama group every winter, head a Noson Lawen party which travelled to give evenings of entertainment in chapel and village halls around Wales, and give unstinting service to chapel and Sunday School.

Charles Williams married, and had six children. His home on the Bodffordd council estate was 'open house'. His was one of the few families in the village to own a television in the early days, and a friend recalls how the sitting room would be full on special occasions, when neighbours would drop in unannounced to view. it was never inconvenient. There was always a warm welcome.

The BBC Repertory company in Bangor was responsible for producing schools' programmes in Welsh, the Welsh Children's Hour, some documentaries and drama. There was plenty of work, and Charles revelled in the opportunities.

His fame was assured with a regular Noson Lawen

WILLIAM CHARLES
WILLIAMS
MBE
(CHARLES PENFFORDD)
Actor · Diddanwr · Digrifwr
1915–1990

Mae hiraeth am gymeriad-gwerinol.
Graenus ei berfformiad:
Am wên glên hiwmor cefn gwlad.
A thonic ei chwerthiniad.
Emrys Deudraeth

*'Actor, entertainer, comic' is how Charles Williams
is remembered at Bodffordd School.*

programme which he presented, its listening figures breaking all records for Saturday night radio. The audience packing the Penrhyn Hall in Bangor, used as a large studio, would rock with gales of laughter at Charles' own homespun brand of humour.

He was an actor who had never received any formal stage training. His ability was instinctive. He was one of the most able and successful character actors Wales has produced. As one of his colleagues said of him, 'His experience was his training', as throughout the years he created a gallery of country characters purely through keen observation. He understood how to create a character for the ear alone, because he had learned how to listen.

Charles' contemporaries in radio wondered how he would adapt to the very different demands of television drama. Their worries were unfounded. Nobody prepared more carefully. His movement and timing could not be faulted. Many up-and-coming young actors had cause to be grateful for Charles' generous advice, given gently and courteously, and he was never too busy to spare them time to discuss a problem and find a solution.

The soap opera Pobol y Cwm made him the most popular television actor of his day, when he played the part of an elderly resident in an old people's home, often at odds with some of the more awkward inmates, often pouring oil on troubled waters. It was a characterisation which called for both humour and pathos.

Charles Williams never forgot his roots, or his early days. One of his co-actors from the Bangor BBC repertory days called him 'an out-of-the-ordinary, ordinary man'.

One of his contemporaries, writing in his memorial book published after his death at the age of 75 in 1990, remembered actress Ellen Terry's belief that an actor needs imagination, industry and intelligence. Charles Williams, she wrote, had all three. He was the Welsh Spencer Tracey.

Charles became a Member of the Order of the British Empire. The photograph of him with his award outside Buckingham Palace shows him as a short, stocky figure in morning suit and top hat. Although appreciative of the honour, it is safe to guess that he could not wait to change into more customary clothes, return to Bodffordd and carry on life where he belonged.

Anglesey, his home, the family and his environment were the pivot of Charles Williams' success.

# Francis George Fisher (1909-1970)

An Anglo-Welshman who learned to speak and write in Welsh became a prominent figure in Anglesey drama circles in the post-war years. He was the catalyst for the opening of Theatr Fach in Llangefni, an institution which has existed for around 50 years and shows every sign that it is here to stay.

George Fisher was born in Bargoed in South Wales. He won a county scholarship to read mathematics at Cardiff University college. His first post after graduating was in a missionary school in West Africa, but illness cut short his stay there and he had to return home.

While at university, he had begun to write. During his last year, as well as working for a degree, he found time to write a novel, One Has Been Honest, which was published in 1930. After returning from Africa to recuperate from his illness, a friend offered him the use of a cottage so that he could concentrate on writing a second novel. This he did, but his publisher wanted amendments which George Fisher was not prepared to make, so it never appeared.

By this time his health had improved, and he was ready to take up teaching again. He applied for the post of mathematics teacher at Llangefni County School and so was introduced to Anglesey. Here he met and married another member of staff, English teacher Margaret Haslam, and the couple settled down to a busy life in Llangefni.

But the Second World War changed George Fisher's tack once again, and he joined the Navy in 1940. Part of his service was spent in the North Atlantic, where off-duty periods could have been boring but for the fact that this was when he decided to learn Welsh. He had the three Welsh Made Easy books by Caradar sent out to him, and within two years he had mastered the language merely by studying the books and writing regularly to the author, sending his exercises and receiving regular criticism and encouragement.

All the while George Fisher continued to write for magazines and – a new venture – for the stage. His first play was performed at Swansea Little Theatre. Once he could write competently in Welsh, a wide scope opened for his talents. He competed in poetry and drama at the 1943 National Eisteddfod in Bangor, and some of his one-act plays were published. When he was demobilised and back home in Llangefni, George Fisher began to produce plays for the Llangefni Dramatic Society.

The years between 1949 and 1955 were productive for George Fisher. He wrote more plays for competitions; he was a town councillor for three years; he enjoyed sailing his boat around the Anglesey coast; and he was an excellent maths teacher to many county school pupils. But his main leisure-time occupation was theatre.

Llangefni Dramatic Society had been re-established after the war, and the society had been able, thanks to George Fisher's influence, to use the school hall for its private drama presentations. Llangefni Town Hall was used for public performances.

The old swimming bath at school was used as a store for scenery and props, and when the new school building was opened in 1953 the society was allowed to use the physics laboratory in the old school.

Then a blow fell. In 1954 the county education committee announced its intention to pull down the old school and so it appeared that the Dramatic Society would be without a home.

But fate stepped in, in the guise of Llangefni Town Council who took over the Pencraig estate, the house, out-buildings and grounds, and George Fisher saw the chance to realise a dream. The society could create its own little theatre by renting the barn which they would renovate for the purpose. The Town Council agreed, and it was let to the society at a peppercorn rent.

In May 1955, after months of settling problems and physical effort, there was no disguising George Fisher's excitement and pride when the curtain rose on the first production, to a full, appreciative house of 63. By 1957 success was assured, and the auditorium was enlarged to hold 110. There has since been further refurbishment.

George Fisher was an organiser, good at winning co-operation for a venture. He believed in perfecting stage-craft and presentation. He maintained there was still a place for the more homely plays in an area like Anglesey, but he also pushed company and audiences alike to appreciate better class drama. Llangefni's Theatr Fach was one of the few little theatres in Wales which staged plays in Welsh and English.

His efforts towards improving drama in Anglesey and in Wales were the reason for his award of the M.B.E. in 1958. A reflection on the quality of his work came in 1960 when the Gulbenkian Trust awarded Theatr Fach £2,000.

George Fisher died suddenly while producing one of his own plays.

# Percy Ogwen Jones (1894-1982) and Bedwyr Lewis Jones (1933-1992)

Percy Ogwen Jones and Bedwyr Lewis Jones – a father well known in newspaper circles, and his son who tipped scales at university in favour of the Welsh language. Both had their roots in Llaneilian.

Percy Ogwen Jones worked on the land at home in Llaneilian before entering Clynnog College where he intended to spend two years preparing for university entrance. But the first world war put paid to any further education.

He registered as a conscientious objector, and was imprisoned in Dartmoor for three years and two months before returning to work on the land in Anglesey. Here he became interested in trade unions and joined the Labour party.

After another stint in prison he decided to look for newspaper work and went to Cardiff as a proof reader on the Western Mail. By this time, journalism had caught hold of him, and when the opportunity came to set up a Welsh Labour newspaper, Y Dinesydd, in Caernarfon, Percy Ogwen Jones took up the challenge and stayed there for five years. This was followed by a time gaining experience on a national daily, The Daily Herald, in London and Manchester.

He returned to Wales to help introduce Y Cymro in Wrexham where he stayed until 1938 before ending his newspaper career with Y Faner in Denbigh.

When he retired from the newspaper world he returned to Anglesey to farm. He was elected county councillor in 1942 and served for many years. He was also on the University Council and the Joint Education Committee for Wales, supporting

*At Penysarn, on the wall of the school he attended, is the plaque to Bedwyr Lewis Jones, 'teacher, and benefactor of our language'.*

movements promoting youth and the Welsh language.

Percy Ogwen Jones' son, Bedwyr, was born while his father worked with Y Cymro in Wrexham. The family returned to Llaneilian when he was five, and the young Bedwyr attended Penysarn school, then Amlwch County School. There was no sixth form in Amlwch in those days, so he had to travel to Llangefni each day for two years, where he won a scholarship to read Welsh at the university college in Bangor in 1956.

After graduating, Bedwyr Lewis Jones spent two years researching at Jesus College, Oxford, and took up his first teaching post at a small school, Ysgol y Gader, Dolgellau, which had only eight staff. This, he said, was where he learned his teaching skills.

He returned to Bangor in 1959 as assistant lecturer in the

Department of Welsh, becoming head of that department in 1974 on the death of Professor Melville Richards. His influence on the status of the Welsh language in the university was to be his great contribution to education in Wales.

Bedwyr Lewis Jones' rapport with students brought a breath of fresh air into their college life. He made a point of knowing each personally. Remembering a name was all-important. He led an exceptionally busy life, lecturing, continuing with research and, in his own words, doing all he could to 'take the college out to the people' by means of society lectures, his widely popular radio talks where his vitality shone through, and adjudicating at eisteddfodau.

His interests were wide. Although the language and literature of Wales filled the greater part of his life, he made time for sport, he was interested in craft, the social sciences, politics and philosophy and was a staunch supporter of the National Eisteddfod.

He would throw himself whole heartedly into a project. At college students found him to be demanding, but not without sympathy when the occasion arose, and he was always ready with his time if it would result in improved standards.

As an academic, he had the ability to convey knowledge dramatically, easily, with an infectious enthusiasm.

Wherever Celtic languages were of interest, worldwide, he was a popular figure. Immediately before his sudden death he was preparing a lecture to be delivered a fortnight later to an international conference in Jutland, on the subject of the Welsh nation today, healthy in spite of problems to exist throughout its history, and its confidence in the future.

Bedwyr Lewis Jones is remembered by a plaque at Penysarn school.

# Colonel the Hon. Stapleton-Cotton (1849-1925)

An old photograph exists showing a number of women workers, poorly dressed, grouped around a portly gentleman wearing a loud-check tweed suit and cap to match. They were women who made rush mats at Newborough.

The man was Colonel Stapleton-Cotton who lived at Plas Llwyn Onn, Llanedwen, on the estate of his nephew, the 4th Marquess of Anglesey. During his time on the island he encouraged the industry of mat-making from the tough marram grass which grows on the sand dunes at Llanddwyn, and in 1913 set up the Newborough Mat-makers' Association which provided a means to sell the products more widely as a co-operative industry.

Marram grass is a tough, sand-binding plant with coarse leaf-blades which were harvested, bleached in stooks, and when judged ready for working the leaves could be plaited in long lengths. These were sewn together to make mats to cover haystacks.

Marram was also used to make nets for trapping rabbits, and ropes for tying down the mats over the haystacks. Brooms and besoms were also made, along with kneeling mats, floor mats and matting for mattresses for box beds.

Mat-making was a cottage industry, disorganised until the Colonel's efforts to regulate it proved successful.

This was only one of his interests, for he was a local benefactor in many ways; the type of figure who was valuable to a community as organisation was his forte.

He attempted to boost the economy by establishing a successful bacon factory at Llanfair Pwllgwyngyll, an egg-collecting depot alongside the railway, a chicory farm, and a bulb farm.

Colonel Stapleton-Cotton came to Anglesey on retirement from the army after an adventurous career in the Zulu War in South Africa, where he was paralysed in the lower part of both legs when his tent was struck by lightning. But he did not allow his disability to prevent his living a full life.

He was one of the foremost workers in the co-operative effort in agriculture in north Wales, serving on various committees. He was also dominant in military tribunals. And he was a member of the University College Council in Bangor.

Nearer to home, he wrote a practical gardening guide for cottagers to persuade them to make the most of their kitchen gardens and so improve their standard of living. And in his spare time he used local Welsh wool to knit garments which were eagerly sought after by the more fashionable ladies of Anglesey and north Wales society.

All these activities were conducted from his wheelchair.

His main claim to fame, however, was that he was the man behind the Women's Institute movement in Britain. The first branch was opened in Llanfair Pwllgwyngyll in 1915. The branch meets to this day in the corrugated iron building (a First World War ex-army hut from the Kinmel camp), next to the toll-house in the village. The first members made him and his dog, Tinker, who accompanied him everywhere, honorary members.

Colonel Stapleton-Cotton's wife died in 1924, and he decided to emigrate to St John's, Antigua, where he owned a sugar plantation. To bid their well-respected benefactor farewell, his many friends and colleagues in north Wales bought him a motor car. He underwent surgery for a leg amputation, which was successful, and it was hoped that the car would facilitate his new life on the other side of the world.